D0604228

TO The KID IN The PEW

60 Chapel Talks
Series C

ELDON WEISHEIT

Publishing House
St. Louis   London

Note: Scripture passages are quoted from the Today's English Version of the New Testament. Copyright © American Bible Society 1966, 1971.

Concordia Publishing House, St. Louis, Missouri
Copyright © 1976 Concordia Publishing House
MANUFACTURED IN THE UNITED STATES OF AMERICA

Library of Congress Cataloging in Publication Data (Revised)

Weisheit, Eldon.
    To the kid in the pew.

    1. Children's sermons. I. Title.
BV4315.W375   252'.53   74-4548
ISBN 0-570-03238-5 (v. 1)

5 6 7 8 9 10 11 12 13 PP 89 88 87 86 85 84

Preface

I carried a sack of breakfast cereal as I walked into the office of a church where I had been preaching as a substitute for several weeks.

"What's the matter, Pastor?" asked one of the church officers. "Didn't you have time for breakfast this morning?"

"Don't you recognize a sermon when you see one?" another member of the parish answered in my place.

And he was right. The cereal was a sermon—for those who are used to seeing as well as hearing a sermon. The homilies in this book were prepared to help pastors and teachers deliver the Gospel of Christ via eyes as well as ears.

The objects used are not sacred relics. Their value is that they come from the everyday activities of the hearers—children, but also adults who listen in. When the power of Christ's redemption is verbally preached with a visual object, the hearer will have an aid in understanding and remembering the message. As the cross and fish have become visual proclamations of Christ, in a lesser way the objects used in sermons become reminders of a message from God for those who have seen as well as heard a sermon.

The sermons in this book with "The Word" and "The World" are to be thought starters for others who want to share the message of Christ. The one preaching or teaching has the responsibility to apply the message to the hearers. Sometimes the object should be changed to be more a part of the life of the hearers. In all cases the words and feelings should be adjusted to fit the style and faith of the one giving the message. But the message of Christ's love and forgiveness is good for all times and places.

A special thanks to the members of Emmaus Lutheran Church, Dorsey, Ill., where most of these sermons were first preached.

Eldon Weisheit

Scripture Index

The homilies in this book are based on portions of the Epistles selected by the Inter-Lutheran Commission on Worship, Year C.

Dedicated to
my son Tim,
on his 16th birthday,
in appreciation for the joy he has added
to my life.

Contents

Prepare the Way for Love

The Word

May our God and Father Himself, and our Lord Jesus, prepare the way for us to come to you! May the Lord make your love for one another and for all people grow more and more and become as great as our love for you. 1 Thessalonians 3:11-12 (From the Epistle for the First Sunday in Advent)

The World

A bowl filled with water, a bottle with a small opening, and a funnel, all on a large tray.

Today's Bible reading is a prayer for us. Listen to it and think how we need to use this prayer: "May our God and Father Himself, and our Lord Jesus, prepare the way for us to come to you! May the Lord make your love for one another and for all people grow more and more and become as great as our love for you."

Paul wanted to show his love for the people who received his letter. But he needed God's help to find a way to express that love. Paul knew that those people wanted to love others. But they also needed help in finding a way to share love.

We are like Paul and those people. We want to love others. And we want to be loved. But we are not always able to give our love. And we are not always willing to receive love from others.

At times we are like this bowl filled with water and other people are like this bottle. When we want to pour the water into the bottle, it spills. And when we want to give our love, it is misdirected and lost. At other times we are like the bottle, when we cannot receive love from others. That's why we need the prayer in our Bible reading.

And the prayer tells us the way God solves this problem. It asks Jesus to prepare the way for us to give and to receive love.

9

Jesus is like a funnel. When I put the funnel in the bottle, the water can easily be poured from the bowl to the bottle. (Do it.) But notice both the bowl and the bottle needed the funnel. Both those who want to give and those who want to receive love need Jesus.

First God is like the bowl filled with love for us. But we rejected that love. So He sent Jesus to prepare the way for His love to come to us. Jesus funneled all of God's love into our lives.

Now we are like the bowl. We are filled with God's love. But we also need Jesus to prepare the way for us to love others. We can give our love through Him.

As we pray for Christ's coming to earth, we pray that He might come to prepare us to receive God's love. And we pray that He will prepare us to share that love with others.

The Gift Is Inside the Box

The Word

I am sure of this: that God, who began this good work in you, will carry it on until it is finished in the Day of Christ Jesus....Your lives will be filled with the truly good qualities which Jesus Christ alone can produce, for the glory and praise of God. Philippians 1:6, 11 (From the Epistle for the Second Sunday in Advent)

The World

Three identical gift boxes. Box A filled with Christmas cookies. Box B with wadded paper. Box C with eggshells, potato peelings, or other garbage.

Our Bible reading promises you something. It says, "Your lives will be filled with the truly good qualities which Jesus Christ alone can produce." Has God kept that promise for you? Are you filled with good qualities?

We all have to admit that we have bad qualities in us. The bad in us shows in some of the things we do and say. Yet God has promised to fill us with good. Let's use these three Christmas boxes to help us understand how God is keeping His promise. The boxes all look alike. It seems like it would make no difference which one you would choose as a gift.

But if you look on the inside you will see they are very different. This one (box C) contains garbage. You wouldn't want it as a Christmas gift. Look, this one (B) is carefully packed with paper. It must have something valuable in it. But, no, it has nothing but packing paper. However, this box (A) has Christmas cookies in it. It would be a good gift for any of us. Even though the boxes look the same on the outside, they are different on the inside.

And we are like these boxes. We may all look alike on the outside, but we have different qualities on the inside. Inside we

11

may have bad qualities, like this box. Or we may be filled with nothing, when we want to do neither right nor wrong, when we don't want to hurt people but we don't want to help them either. That is being like this box (B). Or we can be filled with good qualities, like this box (A). We can have something worthwhile to give to others.

If you look at the inside of your life, you may decide you contain something from each of the boxes. You have some bad qualities. Sometimes you don't seem to care about anything or anyone. And yet sometimes you do have good qualities. But if we mix all these together in one box, the bad would destroy the good. I wouldn't want to eat cookies that were mixed with things from this box (C).

To solve that problem, let's listen to the rest of the Bible reading: "I am sure of this: that God, who began this good work in you, will carry it on until it is finished in the Day of Christ Jesus." God has started putting good in you. He has given you love, kindness, and understanding. Because He has started this good work in you, He is keeping that promise to fill you with good qualities. And He also promises that He will keep on filling you with good things. He will forgive the wrong you do. He will help you fight against selfishness. He will help you do good.

We celebrate Christmas each year to remind ourselves that God does not give up on us. He has started a good work in us, and He will keep on giving good to us. Our bad will not destroy the good God gives. Instead, the good will shove out the bad.

Rejoice with the Joy That Lasts

The Word

May you always be joyful in your life in the Lord. I say it again: rejoice! Show a gentle attitude toward all. The Lord is coming soon. Philippians 4:4-5 (From the Epistle for the Third Sunday in Advent)

The World

A set of Christmas tree lights with the following bulbs: green, red, yellow, and a burned-out blue bulb; a small white paper sack.

Be happy! Have a good time! Enjoy life! Our Bible reading for today tells us to rejoice. And to make sure we get the message, St. Paul repeats himself. He says, "I say it again: rejoice!" Christians, like others, sometimes have a problem about being happy. Some are not happy and feel guilty about it because they think they should be—especially at Christmastime. Others are afraid to be happy. Let's take St. Paul's advice and rejoice—not only at Christmastime but all the time.

To see ways we can rejoice, we'll let this sack represent you. The sack is your life, and you are to fill it with joy. Think of the empty sack and put the things that make you happy in it. Then you can see what makes you rejoice.

Some people fill their lives with the wrong kind of rejoicing. They are happy because others have problems. They celebrate when they get something that others don't have. (Put the lighted green light in the sack.) Their lives look like this. The light makes them rejoice, but it is a green light, a jealous light. Their joy is selfish. They want happiness only for themselves. They look for a good time without thinking about others.

Think of other things that make people happy. Happiness is playing with friends, getting good grades or doing a job well, enjoying a joke, seeing something beautiful. Such things that make us happy make us look like this. (Place lighted red light in the sack.) Red is a party color—like balloons, candles, and ribbons. All people can have this kind of happiness. The problem with party happiness is that it doesn't last. When the fun is over, the happiness is gone. Temporary happiness is okay. But it doesn't give us the joy that St. Paul talks about in our Bible reading.

Because some joy is wrong and other joy is only temporary, some people feel it is wrong to be happy. They put this kind of bulb in their lives. (Put burned-out bulb in the sack.) They show no happiness at all. The only thing they enjoy in life is being unhappy. But Christians have a reason to be happy. We celebrate Christmas because we see what God has done to end unhappiness. He wants us to rejoice with Him and the angels. In case you didn't get it the first time, I say it again: God wants you to rejoice.

The Bible reading tells us how. It says, "Show a gentle attitude toward all. The Lord is coming soon." Our joy is like this bulb (yellow). It is a beacon light that guides us and others to the Source of our joy—Jesus Christ. We are happy because He came to be our Savior. We are happy because He is with us now. We are happy because He will come again to take us to heaven.

Our joy in Christ shoves out the jealous joy of selfishness. We can show a gentle attitude toward all because Christ came for all people. Our joy in Christ adds meaning to the everyday temporary joys of life. We can enjoy our daily living without being afraid they will end soon. The Lord is coming. The future is bright.

As Christians we don't have to pretend we are happy. Each one of us has problems. But we have a joy that is greater than any of our problems. If we are sad, remember the Lord is coming. He will rescue us. If we are happy, we can enjoy our happiness knowing that Christ is with us.

Jesus Tells Us Why He Is Coming

The Word

For this reason, when Christ was about to come into the world, He said to God, "You do not want sacrifices and offerings, but You have prepared a body for Me." Hebrews 10:5 (From the Epistle for the Fourth Sunday in Advent)

The World

A wrapped Christmas gift — a game or cookies for a child. A similar wrapped box with the bottom missing.

Suppose I called you on the phone and told you I was coming to your house to see you tomorrow. But I did not tell you why I wanted to talk to you. You would wonder about it, wouldn't you? You might think I was coming to give you a gift. Or you might think I was going to ask you to do some work. Or you might think I was coming to blame you for something you did wrong. You wouldn't know for sure until I got there and told you the purpose of my visit.

As we wait for Christ's coming at Christmas we may also wonder why He is coming. Some may think Christ is coming to earth to blame us for our sins. Others may think He has work for us to do. Others see Him coming to give us a gift.

Jesus tells us why He is coming. Listen to the Bible reading: "For this reason, when Christ was about to come into the world, He said to God, You do not want sacrifices and offerings, but You have prepared a body for Me." Christ told us why He was coming. He was coming in a human body to be a sacrifice for our sins. He came not to blame us for our wrong but to forgive us. He does have a job for us to do, but first He does a job for us. He makes us belong to God so we can live with Him and serve Him.

In the Old Testament the people offered animal sacrifices for their sins. They knew the animals couldn't pay for the wrong they had done, but the sacrifices were a reminder to them that the payment had to be made. Christ told the people He came not to be a reminder that their sins must be paid for. Rather He came to be the Payment.

Look at these two wrapped packages. They look almost alike. But they are different. This one is a gift. See, many of you would like to receive this gift. But this one is only a reminder of a gift. The reminder could be used in a store window or under a tree to make people remember to buy a gift for someone. But the empty box would not be a real gift.

Jesus tells us that He came not to remind us we need a Savior but that He came to be the Savior. We don't have sacrifices of animals in our church today. But we do have other reminders. The music in our worship makes us think of God. The windows remind us of His beauty. The cross and altar remind us He died for us. The flowers remind us He is alive. The candles remind us He is the Light of the world. Our offerings remind us of the blessings He has given us.

Like the sacrifices, all of these reminders serve a purpose. But don't confuse them with the real thing. Christ is God's Gift to us. He came in a human body to give Himself to be our Savior. We come to church not just to hear the music and see the reminders. We come to meet Christ Himself. He tells us that He comes to be with us. And we are here with Him.

Today You Can See God's Gifts

The Word

But when the kindness and love of God our Savior appeared, He saved us. It was not because of any good works that we ourselves had done, but because of His own mercy that He saved us through the washing by which the Holy Spirit gives us new birth and new life. Titus 3:4-5 (From the Epistle for Christmas Day)

The World

Two pieces of clear glass or plastic. (Suggestion: Use overhead projector transparencies.) Trace an outline picture of Christ on one.

Do you realize the most important gifts you received on this Christmas Day are all invisible? You may have received many toys, lots of money, or too much food. But your greatest gifts come from God. And His gifts cannot be seen. He gives us love, kindness, mercy, forgiveness, peace, hope, and more. None of these can be wrapped in packages and delivered. Yet all are real. Our gifts from God are like this transparency. It is not completely invisible, but it is difficult to see. I can put it on the wall and you probably wouldn't notice it unless I showed you where it was. In the same way, God's gifts to us can be seen if you know where and how to look for them.

And our Bible reading tells us how to see those gifts. It says, "But when the kindness and love of God our Savior appeared . . ." There was a time when God's gifts became visible. Almost 2,000 years ago a baby born in Bethlehem changed the world. He delivered all those gifts from God to all people. The Bible reading mentions kindness and love. It also says God saves us. Our salvation includes many other gifts from God. All those invisible gifts became visible in Jesus Christ.

Love is not just an idea. It is a way to live. Love is the way God

17

has given us eternal life. Love is the way He gives us to live with one another. Peace is not just a word on a Christmas card. Peace is the way our lives can be because Christ has removed the conflict of sin. And all the other gifts God has for you today and every other day are real because Christ made them real in your life. In your baptism Christ became a part of your life. Because He started a new life 2,000 years ago, you have a new life today.

God's gifts now look like this (show other transparency). When we need to see God's love, mercy, and that long list of gifts from God, we look to Christ. When Christ (who is God) became a human, He became a part of all our lives. Look at all your Christmas celebration through this transparency. See your gifts, your dinner, your family through this transparency and you see how God's gifts can be a part of your daily living.

And when others think God's gifts are still invisible or even unreal, show them Christ. Help them see the world through Christ, who has shared in this life on earth. Help yourselves and others see how Christ is a part of your daily living. And whenever you or others are with Christ, you have all the gifts of God. They can be seen because Christ has appeared to us.

Why Should Jesus Risk Death?

The Word

Since the children, as He calls them, are people of flesh and blood, Jesus Himself became like them and shared their human nature. He did so that through His death He might destroy the Devil, who has the power over death, and so set free those who were slaves all their lives because of their fear of death. Hebrews 2:14-15 (From the Epistle for the First Sunday After Christmas)

The World

Two kinds of breakfast cereal (one a bite-size piece, the other a box of small grain, not flakes), a plastic sack with a bottom corner cut out so small cereal will pour through but the bite-size piece will not.

Suppose you wanted to store some breakfast cereal in this bag. You pour the cereal in. But look what happens. There is a hole in the bottom of the sack. The cereal falls out the hole. It would be foolish to put cereal in a bag like this. Instead of storing it, you would be throwing food away. That is wasteful.

From one point of view it also seemed wasteful for God to let His Son be born as Jesus, the Baby of Bethlehem. All people who are born will die. When Jesus was born, He accepted the possibility of dying. Our Bible reading says, "Since the children [that's us], as He calls them, are people of flesh and blood, Jesus Himself became like them and shared their human nature."

The hole in this bag is like death. We are born when we come into life (put more cereal in the top of the sack), and we die when we fall out the bottom (let the cereal go out through the hole). For Jesus to come into our life with us seems like a waste, because He will have to die like us.

But wait. Jesus is different. This (piece of bite-size cereal) is also cereal. In some ways it is like the other cereal. But it is also different. It goes into the sack, but it will not go out the hole. In fact, it plugs up the hole. Now I can pour the other cereal in the sack and it will not fall out.

Christ is like us in many ways. But in other ways He is different. He faced death, but death did not destroy Him. Listen to what the Bible reading says: "He did so that through His death He might destroy the Devil, who has the power over death, and so set free those who were slaves all their lives because of their fear of death."

If we were to live by ourselves, we would always have to be afraid of dying—like the cereal in the sack that might fall out of the hole at any time. But when Christ comes into life with us— and remember, that's what Christmas is all about—He plugs up the hole called death. We do not have to be afraid to die, because He is there to protect us. Even when we do die the death that takes us from this earth, we will not fall away from God. Just as Christ died and yet lives, so we can die and still live with Him.

Think of yourself as one of the pieces of cereal in this sack. Remember that Christ came to live in your life with you. See Him as the one who plugs up the hole called death.

A Name to Last All Year

The Word

Through Him [Jesus] God gave me the privilege of being an apostle for the sake of Christ, in order to lead people of all nations to believe and obey. This also includes you who are in Rome, whom God has called to belong to Jesus Christ. Romans 1:5-6 (From the Epistle for the Name of Jesus)

The World

A large calendar for the new year.

Today we start a new year. Many of you have a fresh calendar to replace the old one that ran out of days yesterday.

January 1 is New Year's Day. But remember that January 2 is also a part of the new year. And so is January 3. All of January seems fresh and new on our calendars.

But February is part of the new year too. See—it has the same year listed on it, 19__. In fact, if you look through the calendar you see the same new year listed for every month. January 1, 19__ is New Year's Day because we start the year then. But all the other days and months are also part of 19__. So they are also part of the new year. When we get to December of this year, we will call it the old year. But from that point of view today is part of the old year too, because January and December belong to the same year.

We have just celebrated the birth of Jesus. In a way He is like January 1 of a new year. He is the beginning of a new life. When the Son of God was born in a human family, God became a part of our lives. Eight days after He was born, that would be today the way the Jewish people counted days, He was named Jesus. He was the new life of God on earth.

St. Paul claims that he is also a part of the new life. In our Bible reading he says, "Through Him [that is Jesus] God gave me the privilege of being an apostle, for the sake of Christ." Jesus was the beginning, like the first day of the new year. But Jesus gave His name to others—including Paul. In the name of Jesus, Paul shared the good news of salvation for all people. Through Paul's work the name of Jesus was shared with others. The Bible reading also says, "This also included you who are in Rome, whom God has called to belong to Jesus Christ." Even though the Romans lived a long way from Bethlehem and many years later, they were part of that new life started when Christ was born—like April is part of the same year as January on our calendar.

We also have been given the name of Jesus. His new life is also for us. Though we live far from where He was born and almost 2,000 years later, Christ is still a part of our lives.

From the point of view of Jesus' birth, He is like January 1 and we are way over in December. But just as January and December are both 19__, so we share the name of Jesus with the Baby who was born in the stable, because He became the Savior who gave His life for us.

The Gift That Everyone Received

The Word

Let us praise God for His glorious grace, for the free gift He gave us in His dear Son!... For this reason, ever since I heard of your faith in the Lord Jesus and your love for all God's people, I have not stopped giving thanks to God for you. Ephesians 1:6, 15-16a (From the Epistle for the Second Sunday After Christmas)

The World

Four toy cars (or other Christmas gifts for children that they could use when playing together).

Now is the time for you to write "thank you" notes for Christmas presents—if you haven't already done it. The way you say "thank you" shows how you appreciate a gift.

Suppose your teacher gave you this gift (one car). That is a good gift from a teacher. You have fun playing with it. You are also glad that your teacher thought about you and gave you a gift that you could enjoy.

During Christmas vacation one of your classmates drops by to play with you. The friend has a car just like yours (show second car), and you find that the teacher also gave the car to your classmate. You call some other friends from your class—and discover that they also received the same kind of car as a Christmas gift from the teacher. (Show all the cars.)

You could look at all the cars in two ways. You could say, "My gift isn't so special if the teacher gave the same thing to all the other kids." That way you wouldn't enjoy your gift.

Or you could say, "It's more fun for all the kids from our class to have the same gift because now we can play together. We can have races to see whose car goes the fastest. We can pretend we have a city with a big highway and many cars."

23

God gave all of us the same gift for Christmas. Our Bible reading says, "Let us praise God for His glorious grace, for the free gift He gave us in His dear Son!" We all received the gift of a Savior.

When you discover that God gave you His Son to be your Savior, you might think what a great gift that is. It shows that God loves you very much—you are special. Then you learn that He gave everyone the same gift. Does that make you jealous? Are you less special because God gave the same gift to all others?

Paul was not only glad that he received a great gift from God, but he was also glad that God gave the gift to others. He writes, "For this reason, ever since I heard of your faith in the Lord Jesus and your love for all God's people, I have not stopped giving thanks to God for you."

When Paul thanked God for the gift, he did not just say, "Thanks, God, for saving me." He said, "Thanks, God, for saving others too." That would be like writing a note to the teacher and saying, "Thanks for giving me the car for Christmas. And thanks for giving cars to the others too, because we have more fun playing together."

We can enjoy our Christmas gift from God more because others also have it. The love and forgiveness we have from God belongs to others too. We enjoy it more together.

Safely in the Presence of God

The Word

In union with [Christ], and through our faith in Him, we have the freedom to enter into God's presence with all confidence. Ephesians 3:12 (From the Epistle for Epiphany)

The World

Two cardboard boxes (cracker box size), one about 3" shorter than the other. A cardboard bridge to connect the boxes. Use a 15" by 5" piece of cardboard to make the bridge. Fold 1" up on each long side of the cardboard. Cut a 1" by 3" strip out across the width of the bridge near one end. Several marbles, a tennis ball, and a roll of cellophane tape.

When the Wise Men came to Bethlehem, they came into the presence of God. Because Jesus was God born on earth, those who saw Him saw God. Jesus is also the Way for us to come into the presence of God. Let's use an illustration to see how He brings us to be with God.

Suppose this box (the taller one) is the world, and these marbles are people like you and me. We are in the world. (Put marbles in box.) This other box will represent God. (Place it about 15" from the taller box.) To make it easy for us to get to God we will put this bridge between God and the world. (Place the bridge from the top of one box to the other with the slot near the shorter box.) Now when someone from earth wants to go to God, he or she goes across the bridge. (Roll several marbles down the bridge. Let the children see them fall.) But notice that none of the marbles are getting all the way to God. See why? (Show it.) This slot is an exit for sinners. Because God is holy, no sinner can go into His presence. We can't be guilty and be with God.

If that bridge were the way to get into God's presence, I wouldn't want to go, would you? We can't find a way around the sinners' exit. But don't forget the story of Christmas.

This tennis ball will represent Jesus. He came to live with us on earth. (Place tennis ball in taller box.) He is with us, but He can take the bridge to God. (Roll the tennis ball down the bridge.) Because He is not a sinner, He can go right over the sinners' exit. He can be with us in the world, or He can be in the presence of God.

But now listen to what our Bible reading for today tells us: "In union with Christ, and through our faith in Him, we have the freedom to enter into God's presence with all confidence." We are in union with Christ. That means we are connected to Him. And because we believe in Him we can go into the presence of God with all confidence. That means we don't have to be afraid of the sinners' exit.

It works this way. Because Christ is our Savior, we are united with Him. See how I can make the tennis ball and a marble be in union. (Tape them together.) Now when the big ball rolls down the bridge it carries the marble along with it. The marble also goes over the hole in the bridge. It goes safely into the presence of God.

When you were baptized, you came into union with Christ. Believing in Him, you remain in union with Him. You need not be afraid of being with God. You can go into His presence with all confidence because Christ removes your sin and takes you there.

Does God Treat All People Alike?

The Word

Peter began to speak: "I now realize that it is true that God treats all men on the same basis." Acts 10:34 (From the Epistle for the First Sunday After Epiphany)

The World

Dishes and flatware for a complete place setting for a dinner table.

Today's Bible reading tells us that the apostle Peter was like us in one way. Peter had been told that God treats all people alike. But Peter didn't think it was always true. We may also doubt that God treats all people alike. Take a look around. God made us look different. Some are short and some tall, some black, some white. God lets some people live many years and others die young. Some people are healthy, others ill. Some wealthy and others poor. Do you really think that God treats all people alike?

But listen to what Peter said: "I now realize that it is true that God treats all men on the same basis." God had given Peter a special dream that helped the apostle believe what he had already been told. Let's use an illustration to help us understand the statement that God treats all people alike.

See this place setting. Here is the knife, fork, spoon, plate, glass, cup, and all the things you would need to set the table for a fancy dinner. Each dish and each utensil has a purpose at the dinner. What if I told you that I was going to treat each piece of the table setting alike. That wouldn't work, would it. They each have a different purpose. What if I use the spoon like a knife? Maybe I could spread butter with it, but it wouldn't cut meat. The spoon could be used like a plate. And if I used it like a glass, I

27

wouldn't get much to drink. Obviously, I can't treat all these pieces alike.

But after the meal is over, all of the dishes have to be washed and put away. Then they are treated alike. During our life on earth people also have different purposes, so we are treated in different ways. But God wants to treat us all alike when we leave this earth. He wants to take us all to be in heaven with Him. He has sent His Son to die for all of us. Christ offers to wash us all clean in Baptism. God's way of saving us is exactly alike. If we die as a young baby or an old person, if we have lived with Christ all of our lives or if we learn about Him only a short time before we die, He treats us all alike.

On earth we have different jobs to do, but we are not saved by our work. We have different abilities, but we are not saved by our abilities. But we all have the same love from God through Jesus Christ. And that's what saves us.

When we see only a part of our lives, we may think that God treats us differently. But when we look at all of life we can say with Peter, "I now realize that it is true that God treats all men alike."

The lesson in this for us is to treat people as God treats us. We are also to treat all people alike. We are to recognize Christ's love in others. We are to know that God wants all people to live with Him forever. We are to share that good news with others.

The Spirit Works in Many Ways

The Word

There are different kinds of spiritual gifts, but the same Spirit gives them. There are different ways of serving, but the same Lord is served. There are different abilities to perform service, but the same God gives ability to everyone for their service. The Spirit's presence is shown in some way in each one, for the good of all. 1 Corinthians 12:4-7 (From the Epistle for the Second Sunday After Epiphany)

The World

A book of matches.

(Strike a match and allow it to burn briefly.) Think about the many ways a match can be used. A match makes light. It lights candles, lamps, and flares. A match makes heat. It makes the fire in gas stoves and furnaces, in grills, fireplaces, and bonfires. A match burns things. It can be used to burn leaves or destroy a paper that you want no one else to read.

And the same match can do any of those many jobs. You don't need one kind of match to make light, another to make heat, and yet another to burn something. One match can do all the different things.

While you remember the many things a match can do, listen to the Bible reading for today: "There are different kinds of spiritual gifts, but the same Spirit gives them. There are different ways of serving, but the same Lord is served. There are different abilities to perform service, but the same God gives ability to everyone for their service."

We Christians have many different jobs to do. We must tell other people the good news of Christ. We must teach Christians to learn more about the Gospel. We must help people who are lonely, sick, or have other problems. We must use the love, forgiveness, hope, and other gifts that God has given to us through Jesus Christ. Sometimes we feel we can't do these things. Sometimes we try to do these things by our own power and either fail or do them the wrong way.

But the Holy Spirit gives us the way to do our part in God's kingdom. The Holy Spirit gives us our faith so we know we are not saved by our own efforts because we are saved by what Christ has done for us. Then the Spirit helps us use our faith in our life. We can do all the works of a Christian— not to save ourselves but because we are already saved by Christ.

But we don't all serve God the same way. Just as a match can do many different things in different situations, the Holy Spirit does different work through each of us. St. Paul tells us how the same Spirit gives different abilities for two reasons. First, know what gifts the Spirit has given you. The Bible reading promises: "The Spirit's presence is shown in some way in each one, for the good of all." The Spirit works in you. Know and enjoy the ways you can serve God. Christ loves you. The ways you share that love with others is evidence that the Spirit works in you.

The next reason we need to know that the Spirit gives different gifts is to help us from being jealous of other Christians. If someone has different abilities than you, it does not mean God loves that person more. We are to use the gifts the Spirit has given to us rather than worry about the gifts we do not have. Having certain gifts from the Holy Spirit does not make one Christian more important than another. All gifts are given by God's grace. Because He loves us He gives us ways to serve Him by serving people.

Remember how the match can do many different jobs. The Spirit is like that match. The Spirit gives the power for all work. By His power each of us can share in serving God.

A Look at Our Spiritual Nervous System

The Word

If one part of the body suffers, all of the other parts suffer with it; if one part is praised, all the other parts share its happiness. All of you, then, are Christ's body, and each one is a part of it. 1 Corinthians 12:26-27 (From the Epistle for the Third Sunday After Epiphany)

The World

Several children from the group, a book.

Today's Bible reading talks about the way a physical body works. So we can understand it, I've asked Debbie to help me. First let's see how your body works, Debbie. Can you pick up that book? That was easy. But you used several parts of your body. Now close your eyes so you can't see. (Move the book.) Can you pick it up now? Or let's try another way. Open your eyes, but do not move your arms or hands. Now can you pick it up?

We know how the parts of our bodies work together in almost everything we do. But do you know how all the parts are able to work together? There is a nervous system that connects all parts of the body through our spinal cord and brain. The nerves from the eyes and the nerves from the hand work together to pick up the book. That nervous system keeps all parts of the body aware of the other parts. If you burn your finger, the nervous system sends "ouch" signals to the rest of the body. If someone rubs your back, the nervous system sends "relax" signals to the whole body.

Paul says that we as Christians are like one body. Listen: "If one part of the body suffers, all the other parts suffer with it; if one part is praised, all the other parts share its happiness. All of you, then, are Christ's body, and each one is a part of it." As Christians our spiritual nerve cells are all grafted together like this. (Either ask several other children to join the first so you and

31

all the children can touch finger to finger, or invite the entire congregation to touch fingers so all are united.)

Imagine that our spiritual nervous system is all united. That means one can be the eye and the other can be the hand. One can be the mouth that speaks the message of Christ and the other can be the ear that listens to someone's problems. One can feel pain and all of the rest will know it and do something to help. One can be happy and all the rest will share in that joy.

Not only are we all one body, but Christ is in the body too. He is the head. He came to join us when He was born. Christ's spiritual nerve cells are attached to ours. Through that system we have transferred all our guilt to Him, and He accepts it. When you are wrong or feel shame, remember you are connected to Christ. He removes the problem. Because Christ died and rose again, He has a new life. But He did not let go of us during His death and resurrection. He is still connected to us and we are connected to Him. We share in the joy of His resurrection. We also will share in His resurrection when we are raised from the dead.

Think today how we can help others by being united to them through our spiritual nervous system. Think how others can help us. And always remember that Christ is in the group.

Without Love, We Are Nothing

The Word

I may be able to speak the languages of men and even of angels, but if I have not love, my speech is no more than a noisy gong or a clanging bell. I may have the gift of inspired preaching; I may have all knowledge and understand all secrets; I may have all the faith needed to move mountains — but if I have not love, I am nothing. I may give away everything I have, and even give up my body to be burned — but if I have not love, it does me no good. 1 Corinthians 13:1-3 (From the Epistle for the Fourth Sunday After Epiphany)

The World

A sealed, addressed, and stamped envelope containing blank paper, and a candy box (if near Valentine's Day, heart-shaped) with no candy.

Isn't it fun to get mail? (Show envelope.) And maybe even more fun to get gifts like this one? (Show candy box.) But both the letter and the gift could be a disappointment. Look. (Open the envelope and show the blank pages. Show that the box is empty.) This envelope looked like a letter, but it had no message. The box looked like a gift, but it contains nothing.

Our Bible reading tells us that we too are nothing unless we have love. No matter how well we do our work and no matter how important we become, we are nothing in God's eyes and we cannot enjoy life unless we have love. Love is a necessary part of our lives just as a message is a necessary part of a letter and candy is a necessary part of a box of candy.

You need love two ways. You need others to love you, and you need to love others. God has given you love in Christ. Christ did not die for you because He had to. He could have escaped the judge and the soldiers. Nor did He give Himself to pay for your sins because God the Father made Him do it. He loves you.

Without love His sacrifice would have had no meaning. But with love His death gives you a new life. And this new life is with a God who loves you so much He has died for you.

Since you have received this love, you also have love to give. Unless you have love to give, you do not understand the love you have received. God always gives His love to you so you can enjoy it and share it with others. You know about God's love in Christ because others who have received that love have loved you.

In our Bible reading St. Paul says that if he preached great sermons to people but did not love them, his sermons would be no good. He says if he was wise and clever but didn't love others and wasn't loved by others, his life would be worthless. Even if he died for the sake of the Gospel but had no love, it would be a waste. Love put the message in his letter. Love was the gift he had to give.

Maybe he would write our Bible reading this way for you: "I may be able to get good grades in school and sing like an angel, but if I have not love, my grades are wasted and my singing is filled with static. I may be popular with friends and make everyone laugh at my jokes—but if I have no love, I am nothing. I may go to church every Sunday and give half of my allowance in the offering—but if I have no love, it does me no good."

Add the Gifts Together

The Word

Since you are eager to have the gifts of the Spirit, above everything else you must try to make greater use of those things which help build up the church. 1 Corinthians 14:12 (From the Epistle for the Fifth Sunday After Epiphany)

The World

Six large pieces of paper, numbered 0 through 5, and six children.

The Holy Spirit gives each of us different gifts. Some can sing, some can teach, some can tell others the good news about Jesus, some can speak in tongues, some can help sick people, some can make lonely people happy. Not only do we have different gifts, but we also have different-sized gifts. Some have great gifts, others have small.

So you can see how we are to use our gifts from the Holy Spirit, we will use these numbered cards to illustrate the size of the gifts we have. This card (6) is the largest gift and this one (0) is the smallest. (Give each of the children a card and ask them to hold it over their chests. Have the children stand in front, but do not allow any two to stand side by side.)

You can see that some have greater gifts than others. The one who has the 6 has a gift greater than several of the others put together. Sometimes Christians think they are more important than others because they have greater gifts. Others sometimes feel they are not important because the Holy Spirit has not given them the same kind or the same size gift as others have.

But listen to what our Bible reading for today says: "Since you are eager to have the gifts of the Spirit, above everything else you must try to make greater use of those which help build up the church." The Holy Spirit did not give you your gifts to use only for yourself. When you receive a gift from the Spirit you are

35

blessed, but so also are other people. God blesses others by giving you a gift that you give to others.

Your gifts do not make you more or less important than someone else. We Christians must use our gifts together because we all have the same Savior. When we use the gifts from the Holy Spirit to build up the entire church, the Spirit can do much more work through us.

For example, we might have thought that the children who had 1 and 0 were unimportant. But look what happens if they work together. (Put them side by side to make 10.) See how their small gifts are larger than the 6. Or we can add another person's gifts and see what happens. (Have the child with 2 stand next to the 0.) See, we have a 102. Of course, all Christians can work with others. The more we work with others, the greater our gifts become. The more we divide ourselves from others, the less valuable our gifts become.

Our gifts work together because they come from the same God. When Jesus died for each of us, He also died for all of us. He has blessed us as individuals, and He has also blessed us as people who are united together in His church. He shows His love and power through His people. We can use the gifts He has given us better if we work together with others who also believe in Him.

Think about the gifts you have. And think about the gifts that other Christians have. Put the gifts together, and they will do more to help both you and others.

Look at the New Life in You

The Word

For if the dead are not raised, neither has Christ been raised. And if Christ has not been raised, then your faith is a delusion and you are still lost in your sins. 1 Corinthians 15:16-17 (From the Epistle for the Sixth Sunday After Epiphany)

The World

A paper sack, folded flat, and a balloon that, when inflated, is about the same size as the sack.

When God made us He breathed life into us. We might say we were like this paper sack. (Blow it up.) That's how we are supposed to be as we live with God. But our sin flattened us out. (Mash the sack.) Sin knocked the life out of us. Instead of being filled with life, we have the emptiness of death. Sin also makes it impossible for us to get our life back. (Cut or tear a number of holes in the sack. Make them large enough and in the proper places so the sack cannot be blown back up.) Even though God still loves us after we have sinned, He cannot give us life back in the same way we had it at creation. (Try to blow the sack up.) Our sin has destroyed our life.

But God still loves us. He found another way to take death from us and to give us life again. He sent His Son, Jesus, to be our Savior. This balloon will represent Jesus. (Blow it up.) He also had life from God. But He was willing to give that life up. (Let the air out.) He gave up His life with God to become a part of our lives. That made it possible for Him to become a part of each of us. (Put the balloon in the sack. Keep the opening of the balloon at the opening of the sack.) After Jesus died for us, God raised Him from the dead. Jesus could again have life with God because He had not sinned. (Blow the balloon up while it is in the sack.)

And look what happened—we again have our life restored. Christ can be raised from the dead with a new life. And because Christ is in us, we also are given a new life.

Notice that when I blew up the balloon the sack also was blown up. The two expanded together because one was in the other. Now this is why the resurrection of Christ is so important to us. Unless He rose from the dead, we couldn't be raised from the dead. And if He has risen from the dead with a new life, then all who are with Him will have that new life. Our Bible reading put it this way: "For if the dead are not raised, neither has Christ been raised. And if Christ has not been raised, then your faith is a delusion and you are still lost in your sins."

We cannot just say that Christ rose from the dead, without seeing His new life in our own lives. Our faith is not like this: (Leave the air out of the balloon and remove it from the sack. Mash the sack. Blow up the balloon.) This way we see the resurrection of Christ and say, "That's great! We believe it!" But we don't share in it.

Instead, the resurrection is this way. (Put the balloon back in the mashed sack. Blow up the balloon.) We do see Christ's resurrection. We do believe that He rose from the dead. And because He has a new life, we do too. No longer do our sins hold us in death. No longer do we lose the new life that God gives, through the sinful holes in our own lives. Christ came to be with us to give us a new life. And He remains with us to keep that new life in us.

Raised with New Power

The Word

This is how it will be when the dead are raised to life. When the body is buried it is mortal; when raised, it will be immortal. When buried, it is ugly and weak; when raised, it will be beautiful and strong. When buried, it is a physical body; when raised, it will be a spiritual body. 1 Corinthians 15:42-44a (From the Epistle for the Seventh Sunday After Epiphany)

The World

Two large blocks of wood (or tin cans), a piece of cardboard one inch wide and 12 inches long, and a foot ruler.

One of the many blessings of the resurrection from the dead is that it will give us a new start. In our lives on earth we have sinned and made many mistakes. Because of them we will die. But because Christ has taken the punishment from death, we will be raised from the dead and live again.

Sounds great. But one question bothers many people. What will be so great about coming back to life if we only repeat the same mistakes we did the first time around. The Garden of Eden was a perfect place with no sin. Then Adam and Eve destroyed it by sin. Heaven will also be a perfect place with no sin. Could it be that we will sin in heaven and ruin that place also?

Today's Bible reading says, "No!" When we are raised from the dead we will be given a new kind of life. St. Paul writes: "This is how it will be when the dead are raised to life. When the body is buried it is mortal; when raised, it will be immortal. When buried, it is ugly and weak; when raised, it will be beautiful and strong. When buried, it is a physical body; when raised, it will be a spiritual body."

We'll use an illustration to help understand that reading.

Here is a large canyon. (Place blocks a foot apart.) And here is a bridge over the canyon. (Place the cardboard piece across the gap.) Now suppose that a truck goes over the bridge and breaks it down. (Apply weight to center of the cardboard and push it down.) The bridge is destroyed. Now let's build it back. (Put the cardboard back.) Then another truck going over the bridge will destroy it again. (Push the cardboard down.) So we need to build it back.

You can see that it does no good to continue to rebuild the bridge the same way each time. The fact that a truck could break it down means it has to be built stronger. So we rebuild it this way. (Put the ruler across the span and place the cardboard on top of it.) Now the same weight will not destroy the bridge. It has been rebuilt in a stronger way.

Our death and resurrection are like the breaking down and building up of the bridge. Sin is a load too heavy for us to bear. It destroys us. (Put the cardboard on the blocks again and press it down.) But God will raise us from the dead. However, He will give us a different kind of life. He will add to it. (Put the ruler and cardboard together again.) When we died we were mortal, that is, we were able to die. But we will be raised immortal; that means we will never die again. We had problems that caused our death. When we are raised, we will be free from those problems.

When we die, God does not just restore our lives. He resurrects them. He gives us a new and better life for eternity.

Don't Be Scared of Death

The Word

Death gets its power to hurt from sin, and sin gets its power from the Law. But thanks be to God who gives us the victory through our Lord Jesus Christ. 1 Corinthians 15:56-57 (From the Epistle for the Eighth Sunday After Epiphany)

The World

A picture (that can be removed) in a frame with glass, a marker pencil, glass of water, piece of candy, a wiping cloth.

Many people are afraid to talk about dying. Some won't even use the word death. Our Bible reading tells us why death is a frightening subject. It says, "Death gets its power to hurt from sin, and sin gets its power from the Law."

Death has a power over us because we are sinners. The Bible says the wages of sin is death. Because we are all sinners, we are afraid that payday is coming—a day when all of our sins must be paid for.

Sin gets its power from the Law. Each time we read God's law we see how we have sinned and the threat of death makes us afraid. Yet if we ignore God's law, we still continue to sin and the same threat is over us.

We can compare that threat to ways that this picture could be damaged. (Show the picture outside the frame.) Suppose this picture is important to you. You want to keep it, but you also want to see it and to show it to others. Yet if you put the picture out for everyone to see, it might be destroyed. Someone might accidently mark it with a pencil. (Hold marker pencil but do not mark the picture.) Or someone might spill water on it. Or a piece of candy could get mashed on it. Many things could happen to destroy the picture. Worrying about what might happen could keep you from enjoying the picture.

41

In the same way worrying about sin and death keeps us from enjoying life. If we always worry about dying, we can't enjoy living. The threat of death is the devil's way of blackmailing us. No matter what we do, he can always say, "But I know what you have done wrong. You are going to die."

But listen to something else that our Bible reading says, "But thanks be to God who gives us the victory through our Lord Jesus Christ." Death no longer has any power over us. Sin can't threaten us and ruin our lives. Christ has died for us. He has paid the wages of sin. He has destroyed sin's power over us.

Christ for us is like this frame for the picture. See, when the picture is behind the glass it is protected. If water is spilled on it, a cloth can wipe it off. (Do it.) If a mark is made on the glass or a piece of candy mashed on it, you can clean it off. The glass protects the picture from damage. Now you can keep the picture out where you and others can see and enjoy it.

You can also enjoy living without worrying about sin and death. Christ has removed the threat. When the devil blackmails you with the threat of dying, you can say, "But Christ has already died for me. When I die He will be with me and will raise me up again to live with Him."

If You Don't See the Gospel, Look Again

The Word

For if the Gospel we preach is hidden, it is hidden only to those who are being lost. They do not believe because their minds have been kept in the dark by the evil god of this world. He keeps them from seeing the light shining on them, the light that comes from the good news about the glory of Christ, who is the exact likeness of God. 2 Corinthians 4:3-4 (From the Epistle for the Last Sunday After Epiphany)

The World

Tape the following (from the top only, so each can be lifted) on a large poster paper: A black square, a white disk, a blue triangle. Place a red disk under the black square so it cannot be seen.

Study this poster carefully, because I am going to ask you what you saw on it. (Turn the poster around.) Now, is there a red disk on the poster? I say yes there is. I see most of you saying that there isn't. We could have a debate about the red disk, but the easy way is to look again. See. (Show the front side of the poster.) You may still say there is no red disk. I still say there is. Again we could argue about it. But I am right—see? (Raise the black square.) You couldn't see it because it was hidden. After I've shown it to you, we have nothing to argue about.

Please think about this poster and the hidden red disk as you hear the Bible reading for today: "If the Gospel we preach is hidden, it is hidden only to those who are being lost. They do not believe because their minds have been kept in the dark by the evil god of this world. He keeps them from seeing the light shining on them, the light that comes from the good news about the glory of Christ, who is the exact likeness of God."

Many people do not see the Gospel of Christ. And each of us Christians at certain times may not be able to see it. But our Bible reading says that when we do not see the Gospel, it does not mean there is no Gospel. You couldn't see the red circle. But it was there. We need not argue about whether or not there is a Gospel. The Gospel is the good news that Christ has paid for the sins of the world and that through Him all people can be saved.

Rather than debating with others to make them believe the Gospel, we should see what is keeping them from seeing it. And when we don't see the Gospel's power in our lives, we should find out what is blocking our view. Our Bible reading tells us that the false gods of the world hide the good news of Christ.

We have to know what false gods are hiding the Gospel from us or others. Even if you knew the red disk was under one of the papers on this poster, you wouldn't know which was hiding it until you looked. Let's look to see what might be hiding the Gospel from us.

Greed and selfishness are twin false gods that try to hide the Gospel. When we think only of ourselves and want things to make us happy, we are hiding the Gospel of Christ. We are then looking for something else than His love.

Jealousy and hatred also try to cover the Gospel. When we let anger cover Christ's love, and when we try to hurt other people, we are hiding the Gospel's message of forgiveness.

Look at other areas in your own life that might hide the Gospel from yourself. Consider your daydreams, your goals, your temptations. Don't let these things cover Christ—rather let Him cover them.

And help other people see the Gospel by helping them get rid of the false gods of the world that cover Christ's love for them.

Don't Be Disappointed by Lent

The Word

For the Scripture says, "Whoever believes in Him will not be disappointed."
... As the Scripture says, "Everyone who calls on the name of the Lord will be
saved." Romans 10:11, 13 (From the Epistle for the First Sunday in Lent)

The World

A sealed envelope and a pair of roller skates in a gift box (another suitable
gift for a child of either sex may be substituted).

Have you ever expected a special gift and then been
disappointed? Suppose you had wanted a new pair of roller
skates for your birthday and your parents seemed to agree that
you should have the skates. They even asked what kind you
wanted and checked what size you wore. Then you would be sure
that you would get skates for your birthday.

But when the big day finally arrived, you found this envelope
on your plate. There are no skates in this. When you open it you
read, "Happy birthday. The store didn't have the exact skates
you wanted. Because we didn't want you to be disappointed with
the wrong kind of skates, we ordered a pair for you. They'll be
here next week." Now your disappointment is over. And the next
week you received a special package. (Show skates.) They are the
exact skates you wanted.

Now let's think about a gift that God has promised for us. We
heard about it at Christmas when the angels sang about Jesus'
birth. During the Epiphany season we saw how Jesus showed
that He had God's power and He would use it for our good. So
we know that He will use that great power and love for us.

But Lent comes like a big disappointment. We were expecting
to receive the gift of eternal life from God's Son. Instead, we see
how Jesus is arrested, tortured and finally killed on a cross. After

hearing the happy stories of Christmas and Epiphany, Lent is a sad time.

But listen to what our Bible reading tells us. It has two promises, both from the Old Testament and both repeated in the New Testament. First it says, "Whoever believes in Him will not be disappointed." Even when we see Jesus falsely accused and beaten, we need not be disappointed. Jesus had to take suffering and death for us to give us the gift that He had promised. He did not want to disappoint us by giving us a smaller gift. The second promise tells us for sure what He wants to give us. It says, "Everyone who calls on the name of the Lord will be saved."

Because Christ suffered and died for us, we know He has taken away our sin. He has been punished in our place. When we are in need, we ask Him for help because He has already helped us. He has saved us—saved us from a wasted life on earth and saved us for an eternal life with Him in heaven.

When you feel the sadness and disappointment of Lent, remember this envelope. It tells us that we will receive the gift that God has promised. Lent tells us that God makes sure we get the exact gift we need—a victory over sin and death. Then on Easter, when we celebrate Christ's victory and see Him raised from the grave, we will receive the complete gift (show box of skates) that Christ gives to all people.

Friend or Foe of the Cross?

The Word

There are many whose lives make them enemies of Christ's death on the cross. They are going to end up in hell; because their god is their bodily desires, they are proud of what they should be ashamed of, and they think only of things that belong to this world. We, however, are citizens of heaven. Philippians 3:18b-20a (From the Epistle for the Second Sunday in Lent)

The World

A bottle of aspirin and a cross.

The cross (show it) has an important message for us. It reminds us that Christ died for our sins and rose again so we could live with Him forever. We want all people to know this message, because we want to share our blessing with them.

But in our Bible reading for today, St. Paul tells us we should be concerned, not only about those who do not know the message of the cross, but also about those who misuse the message. He says, "There are many whose lives make them enemies of Christ's death on the cross." We must ask ourselves if we do something that makes us the enemies of Christ's death on the cross and also what we can do to help others who misuse the message of Christ.

Maybe we can understand the problem by using this comparison. See this bottle of aspirin. These pills were made to help us. We keep them in our homes to help anyone who has a headache, toothache, or other pains. The aspirin helps relieve the pain. But taking too many aspirin is dangerous. To misuse the aspirin hurts our lives instead of helping. Aspirin that are intended to help us can actually kill us if we misuse them.

The message of the cross is intended to save us. Yet Paul says that anyone who is an enemy of the cross will go to hell. If we misuse the message of God's love for us, we hurt ourselves instead of receiving the help that Christ offers.

The Bible reading tells us how we can be enemies of the cross. It says, "Their god is their bodily desires, they are proud of what they should be ashamed of, and they think only of things that belong to this world."

The message of the cross not only saves us when we die, but it also changes our lives now. Anyone who tries to use the Gospel as a way to go to heaven without seeing Christ as a part of this life is misusing the cross. For example, we cannot say that because we are forgiven we are free to sin. Christ's forgiveness of our sins does not mean that He approves of what we have done wrong. We cannot put our desires first in our lives if Jesus is the Lord of our lives. Nor can we ask God to forgive our sins at one time and later brag about the same sin.

What do you do if you know you have misused the Gospel? How can you help others who have used Christ's love in the wrong way? Our Bible reading tells us. It says, "We, however, are citizens of heaven." Christ offers forgiveness to us even when we misuse His forgiveness. He still wants to help us. He forgives us again. He gives us another new start.

Because we are citizens of heaven, we know that Christ is with us. He continues to help us. And He also gives us ways to help others. We help them by showing them that we love them and are willing to share Christ's forgiveness with them.

Be Ready to Receive God's Gifts

The Word

I want you to remember, brothers, what happened to our ancestors who followed Moses. They were all under the protection of the cloud, and all passed safely through the Red Sea. . . . All ate the same spiritual bread, and all drank the same spiritual drink. They drank from that spiritual rock that went along with them; and that rock was Christ Himself. But even then God was not pleased with most of them, and so their dead bodies were scattered over the desert. 1 Corinthians 10:1, 3-5 (From the Epistle for the Third Sunday in Lent)

The World

A can of juice, a can opener, two clean drinking glasses, and one glass with milk and cigarette ashes in it.

Here is a can of orange juice—just the right drink for anyone who is thirsty. (Open the can. Pour juice into one of the clean glasses. Take a sip.) That's good. I'll pour one for you. (Pour juice into the dirty glass.) But you wouldn't drink this, would you? In case you didn't notice, the glass had not been washed. It had milk and cigarette ashes in it before I put the orange juice in. The same juice went into both glasses. But one drink turned out good and one turned out bad.

Our Bible reading tells us about about the same problem in people. It says that God gave all of the people who left Egypt with Moses the same gifts. They were all delivered from the enemy army. They all received the miracles of special food and water. They all heard the same message of a Savior. Then it says, "But even then God was not pleased with most of them, and so their dead bodies were scattered over the desert."

Even though they all received the same blessings from God, some were later rejected by Him. Why? If He loved them enough to let them share in His blessings, why were some lost? The answer to those questions are important because later Paul says this story is a reminder for all of us. We all receive many of the same blessings from God. We too have food and clothing. We all have had prayers answered when we were in trouble. God has poured His blessings on all of us. But the Bible reading warns us not to count on those blessings to prove we are God's people.

Before we let such questions scare us and we start to doubt that God loves us, let's remember the orange juice. The same juice was poured into both glasses. In one the juice was good because the glass was clean. In the other the juice was not good because the glass was dirty.

Look at the gifts that God pours into our lives. If our lives are clean, the gifts are a blessing and we use them as gifts from God. If our lives are not clean, the gifts are ruined by our sins. If we are to be ready to receive God's gifts and use them, our lives must be cleaned.

Remember how our lives are cleaned. Christ washes us. Because He has suffered in our place, we are clean; and so we can receive the gifts of God with joy. The Bible reading tells us we cannot be sure we are saved just because we have blessings from God. All of the people who left Egypt with Moses also had blessings from God, but some were lost.

When we know we are like this dirty glass, we do not hide our sin. Instead we ask Christ to make us clean. He washes us clean by His grace. Then we become like this glass. (Show second clean glass.) Then He can pour His blessings into our lives. (Pour juice in the second clean glass.)

Look at the Other Side

The Word

For the message about Christ's death on the cross is nonsense to those who are being lost; but for us who are being saved, it is God's power. 1 Corinthians 1:18 (From the Epistle for the Fourth Sunday in Lent)

The World

With a large darning needle and heavy yarn spell out the words "Jesus Saves" on a poster. Stitch part of the first letter, then a letter at the end of the message, then back to the beginning. Continue so the message can be read from the front of the poster but the back will be a complete jumble.

(Show the back side of the cardboard.) Can you see a message in this? Take a good look at it and tell me what you think it is. I'll tell you, it is not a picture but is a message in words—not Chinese but English. Perhaps it looks like nonsense to you.

But look again. (Turn the cardboard around.) Now you can easily read the message: "Jesus saves." That is the message of the cross. Jesus died to save us from our sins. He rose again to save us for eternal life. The message is easy to read from this side.

At least it is easy for us to read. However, our Bible reading tells us that the message "Jesus saves" is not easy for all people to understand. It says: "The message about Christ's death on the cross is nonsense to those who are being lost; but for us who are being saved, it is God's power."

To some people the message that Jesus saves seems as foolish as the backside of this poster. We can think about all kinds of questions about the cross. We can ask: How can one person die for everyone? Why should anyone have to die for me? How can anything that happened almost 2,000 years ago change things today?

The Bible gives us answers to those questions and to many

other questions people ask. But answering such questions does not always help people see the answer. As long as we are trying to understand everything with our minds, we will have more questions to ask.

To read the message on this poster I had to turn it over to see it from the other side. Sometimes we also have to turn our minds over too and see the message from the other side. Instead of asking questions about the cross, we can see it as the place where we receive answers. The cross tells us God loves us. It gives us the answer to death and to sin because Christ died to take away our sin. The cross answers our questions about the purpose of our lives. Christ not only died to save us from sin; He saved us for something. We are to live for Him today. We are to love whom He loves and help whom He helps.

Remember, it is not wrong to ask questions. We are to use our minds in every way we can. But also remember, we are not saved because we understand the Gospel. We are saved because we trust in Christ.

When others ask questions about the cross, we should be willing to give answers. But our best answer is to show that the cross is a power in our lives. Christ has changed us. We are His people. We can tell others how to be His people too.

Your Hands Are Full, of What?

The Word

I reckon everything as complete loss for the sake of what is so much more valuable, the knowledge of Christ Jesus my Lord. For His sake I have thrown everything away; I consider it all as mere garbage, so that I might gain Christ, and be completely united with Him. No longer do I have a righteousness of my own, the kind to be gained by obeying the Law. I now have the righteousness that is given through faith in Christ, the righteousness that comes from God, and is based on faith. Philippians 3:8-9 (From the Epistle for the Fifth Sunday in Lent)

The World

A cross (about 6 inches long) and a collection of symbols of accomplishment for the hearers' age group; suggestions — report cards, baseball or a trophy, coin bank, jewelry, clothing, souvenirs.

In our Bible reading St. Paul talks about two things in his life that could make him happy. One is the knowledge that Christ is his Savior. We'll use this cross as a symbol of that happiness. The cross reminds us that God loves us and gives us His goodness in Jesus. (Continue to hold the cross in one hand.) When we have Christ, we also have His goodness. That means that even though we have done wrong, we are free because Christ gives us His holiness to cover our wrong.

Then St. Paul says the other kind of happiness would have come from his own goodness. He calls it "a righteousness of my own, the kind to be gained by obeying the Law." Not everything we do is bad. We obey some of the Law and we often think we should get some of the credit. Suppose you get good grades in school, then you'd want to get credit for your hard work; so you'd add this report card to the things that make you happy. (Put report card in hand with the cross.) If you're a good athlete, you might add this (baseball or trophy). If you can earn or save money, you might add this bank. If you have nice jewelry or clothing, you might add them. (Continue to add the symbols collected for your group until the cross in your hand is completely covered.)

Now we've got everything that makes us happy all in one hand. And we've also got the same problem that Paul had. The most important part of our life is hidden. You can't see the cross anymore. It is still there, but it is covered by all the other things in our lives.

We often do cover Christ in our lives. We love Him and we know we need Him as our Savior. But we can also have other things that we love and need. Soon we can start to depend on the things we've done instead of what Christ has done.

When that happened to St. Paul, he said: "For Christ's sake I have thrown everything away; I consider it all as mere garbage, so that I might gain Christ." (Drop everything except the cross.) St. Paul needed to see Christ as the most important part of his life, and he wanted others to see Christ in him. When his life got too cluttered, he got rid of the least important things and said: "I now have the righteousness that is given through faith in Christ, the righteousness that comes from God, and is based on faith."

Our lives may also need a spring housecleaning. All of the other things that were in the hand with the cross are not wrong. But they must not cover Christ in our lives. They can make us happy for a while, but they cannot keep us happy. Keep the message of Christ first in your life. Then your hands will be full— full of His love and forgiveness and full of opportunities to serve Him.

Where Did You Get That Attitude?

The Word

The attitude you should have is the one that Christ Jesus had. Philippians 2:5
(From the Epistle for Palm Sunday)

The World

Eight plastic sandwich bags. One blown up like a balloon and tied shut with a rubber band, one containing colored water and tied shut with a rubber band, one containing a piece of cardboard cut to the size of the bag, one filled with dry cereal, four empty.

Think how you would describe these four items. (Hold up the filled plastic bags, one at a time.) Do you think you could describe these so everyone else would know which one you were talking about?

Now look at these four. (Show the empty bags.) Can you describe each of these so others would know which one you meant? That would be difficult, since they all are exactly alike.

But did you notice the other four are all alike too? They are all plastic sandwich bags. They appear to be different because of what is inside them. Today's Bible reading tells us that we also are different because of what is inside us. It says: "The attitude you should have is the one that Christ Jesus had."

Though our attitudes are inside us, they make us look different on the outside just as what is in these bags makes them look different. You can recognize a person who has a happy attitude or one who has an angry attitude. You can tell a lazy attitude, a sad attitude, or a funny attitude. We are not like these sacks (empty) that all look alike. We have different sizes, shapes, and colors. But much more important for our lives are the different attitudes we have.

The Bible reading tells us we should have the same attitude

that Christ had. In the next sentences it describes some of His attitudes. He was humble. He did not demand that everything go His way. He obeyed the law. From other parts of the Bible we can see other attitudes of Christ that we should have. He had an attitude of love and forgiveness for all people. He wanted to help everyone in need. He was thoughtful and understanding. The attitude you should have is the one that Christ Jesus had.

Notice the Bible reading doesn't tell us to *act* like Jesus. We can't just pretend to be humble or loving or kind. That would only change the outside of our appearance. But when we have the attitudes that Jesus had, we are changed on the inside.

And Jesus gives us His attitudes. When He loves us, He gives us a way to love others. When He forgives us, He gives us a way to forgive others. He gave His life for us so we could have His attitudes.

When someone says to you, "Where did you get that attitude?" ask yourself if it came from Jesus. If not, trade your attitude in for His.

And He Appears Also to Us!

The Word

I passed on to you what I received, which is of the greatest importance: that Christ died for our sins, as written in the Scriptures; that He was buried, and was raised to life on the third day, as written in the Scriptures; that He appeared to Peter, and then to all twelve apostles. Then He appeared to more than five hundred of His followers at once, most of whom are still alive, although some have died. Then He appeared to James, and then to all the apostles. Last of all He appeared also to me. 1 Corinthians 15:3-8a (From the Epistle for Easter Day)

The World

Six small drinking glasses (each half full of water) and a pitcher with enough water (colored green) to fill five glasses. Another supply of clear water, and a towel in case you spill.

St. Paul tells us the most important message for us is that Christ died for our sins and rose again. The green water in this pitcher stands for that message. The green water is the Easter message: Christ has won the victory over death.

This glass with clear water in it stands for Peter on Easter morning. He had denied Jesus. He had not understood Jesus' promise. Yet Jesus came to Peter. (Bring pitcher and glass together.) And Jesus shared the message that He died for sins and rose again. (Fill glass from pitcher.) Now Peter has the message too! He is forgiven. He has eternal life.

Jesus then shared the message with the twelve apostles. (Fill second glass.) Then with 500 people. (Fill third glass.) Then with James. (Fill fourth glass.) Finally, Paul says Christ also came to him. (Empty pitcher in fifth glass.)

We are here to celebrate Easter today. We are glad the disciples, the 500, and Paul saw the risen Savior. But if Easter is to be real for us, we must also see the victory Christ won over death. We are this glass (sixth glass). Has the message lasted 2,000 years for us? Or do we have an empty pitcher this morning?

For us to see Christ today, we need to see what happens to a person who receives the message of Christ's victory over death. Let's start over. (Pour the water from the five glasses back into the pitcher. Fill each glass half full of clear water again.)

When Christ appeared to Peter (pour green water into the first glass), Christ became a part of Peter's life. The change happened because Christ gave His life for Peter. But Peter then gave his life to Christ. From then on Peter shared Christ's ministry of delivering the message of new life. (Pour all the water from the first glass back into the pitcher.) Instead of Peter using up a part of the message, he increased it.

Each time Christ gives the message of victory over death to people (pour from pitcher to four more glasses), they become a part of His ministry (pour water back into the pitcher).

So now the message comes to us. The pitcher is not empty. Through the last 2,000 years the message has grown because many people have lived and died knowing that Christ has given them eternal life. They have received Christ's message and they have passed it on. We do not see the resurrected body of Christ today, but we see how His resurrection changed many people. Christ is alive for us today. The message is real. (Fill the last glass.)

When we know Christ is our Savior, our lives are changed too. We also become a part of Christ as we share His message with others. (Pour water from the last glass back into the pitcher.) We are with Christ now.

Who Can Tell Us How to Live?

The Word

"Don't be afraid! I am the first and the last. I am the living One! I was dead, but look, I am alive for ever and ever. I have authority over death and the world of the dead." Revelation 1:17b-18 (From the Epistle for the Second Sunday of Easter)

The World

Pictures of: Bald man, man with hair; heavy person, thin person, Jesus. (If speaking to a large group, use large poster pictures or an overhead projector.)

If these two people (pictures of bald man and person with hair) were selling a new kind of shampoo that was guaranteed to make hair grow on a bald head, which would you buy from?

Or look at these two pictures (heavy person and thin person). If each of them was selling a program that guaranteed you that you would not be overweight, which would you buy from?

Now look at these pictures (person with hair, thin person, and Jesus.) If one of these people would tell you not to be afraid to die, which one would you believe?

In each case we are talking about authority. A bald person lacks authority to sell shampoo to help you grow hair. An overweight person would have a difficult time selling a weight reduction program. And who can tell us not to be afraid to die? The person who would have the most authority would be the one who had done it. However, those who have died can't tell us about the experience.

Except for Jesus. He died. And He arose again. Now listen to what He says in our Bible reading for today: "Don't be afraid! I am the first and the last. I am the living One! I was dead, but look,

I am alive forever and ever. I have authority over death and the world of the dead."

When Jesus talks to us about death, He is not just sharing His opinions. He is also sharing His experience. He is not saying, "I think that death is okay; so you don't have to be scared." He says, "Don't be afraid. I was dead, but look, I am alive forever and ever."

Because Jesus is an authority on death, He is also an authority on life. He can show us how to live without being afraid of death. He can tell us about life on earth because we will also live with Him forever in heaven.

Think of all the things Jesus has told us to do. He says we are to love one another. We are to help all people who are in need. We are to share the Gospel with everyone. We are to forgive.

Jesus has the authority to tell us such things. He has the authority, not just because He has the power, but because He has the way of life. He has lived, and died, and lives again. We must make all of our decisions by looking back and seeing what has happened to us before. Then we see our mistakes and our faults and we are afraid. But in Christ we can look ahead. We can make our decisions on the basis of what He has promised us. And He knows what He is talking about.

Watch What You Throw Away

The Word

Again I looked, and I heard angels, thousands and millions of them! They stood around the throne, the four living creatures, and the elders, and sang in a loud voice: "The Lamb who was killed is worthy to receive power, wealth, wisdom, and strength, honor, glory, and praise!" Revelation 5:11-12 (From the Epistle for the Third Sunday of Easter)

The World

An old dish and a price tag. (Any other "antique" may be substituted.)

When it comes time for spring housecleaning many mothers ask their children to help with the work. Housecleaning includes sorting out the junk that collects in basements, attics, and storerooms. If you were helping sort a box of stuff and you found this dish, what would you do with it? The dish is chipped. The rest of the set has been either broken or lost. So you might as well throw this one away too. Right?

Suppose you did throw it away. Then later as you walked past an antique shop you saw the same dish in the window. But this time it has a price tag on it. You look at the tag. It says, $25. Just imagine—the store is asking $25 for a dish that you threw away.

Something like this happens in the story of Lent and Easter. Remember what the religious people of that day said when Pilate asked what he should do with Jesus. They said, "Crucify Him! Crucify Him!" And Pilate gave in to them. Jesus was killed.

But today's Bible reading tells us what happened after Christ was crucified. This time we get a peek into heaven. Again we see Jesus surrounded by a big crowd. Only this time it is a crowd of angels. And they are saying something very different than the crowd in Jerusalem. They sing: "The Lamb who was killed is worthy to receive power, wealth, wisdom, and strength, honor, glory, and praise!" Some people may have thrown Christ out on earth. But in heaven He receives the highest honor and glory.

We can easily say that we want to be like the angels and not like the people who saw no value in Christ. But let's make sure we understand the lesson by applying it to our lives.

For example, Jesus told us to tell others about Him as the Savior of the world. Do you throw out His instruction as though it **was** worthless? Or do you give it a top place in your life?

What do you do with the things Jesus said about helping people in need? Remember, He said if you give a hungry person food, you are feeding Him. If you help a sick person, you are helping Him. Do you refuse to help Jesus by helping others as though it were not necessary? Or do you praise Jesus by giving His love and help to others?

Keep on Growing

The Word

"These are the people who have come safely through the great persecution. They washed their robes and made them white in the blood of the Lamb. That is why they stand before God's throne and serve Him day and night in His temple. He who sits on the throne will protect them with His presence. Never again will they hunger or thirst; neither sun nor any scorching heat will burn them; because the Lamb, who is in the center of the throne, will be their shepherd and guide them to springs of living water. And God will wipe away every tear from their eyes." Revelation 7:14b-17 (From the Epistle for the Fourth Sunday of Easter)

The World

A ripe fruit and a blossom from a fruit tree. (If not available, use pictures.)

Our Bible reading for today tells us about people who are praising God. In one way we are with them. We also are here to sing our thanks to Christ, the Lamb who has taken away our sin.

But there is a difference between us and those described in the Bible reading. They are already in heaven. They have survived the problems of earth. Now they are with God, and He protects them from all problems. He has wiped away their tears. They will not thirst, hunger, or suffer again.

But we will live with problems. We still have hurts and pains—not only in our bodies, but also in our minds and souls. We have worries and fears. We have guilt and sorrow. But we also have a Savior—a Savior who has helped others through all the problems of life and taken them to be with Him in heaven. And He has promised to do the same for us.

We can compare ourselves to this fruit blossom. See, there is a tiny fruit already forming on the branch. It will have to grow a long time before it becomes ripe like this one. During that time a freeze might destroy it. Wind might blow it from the tree. Worms might eat their way into it. If any of those things happen, the blossom will not become a ripe fruit.

We are already Christians. The Holy Spirit has given us faith in Christ as our Savior. But we are still growing. Many persecutions will try to make us fall from the church. Some will laugh at us for loving God. We will sometimes think we are good enough by ourselves and that we don't need God. At other times we will think we are so bad that He couldn't want us. We will be selfish and hateful, greedy and lustful.

But we can survive. The same power of Christ that made us blossom into faith will keep us in faith. God does love us. Christ has died for us. He is alive now. All of this is to give us power to overcome the problems of life.

Remember the people in the Bible reading. They are like this ripe fruit. They survived the persecutions of life. They now praise God forever. And we can too.

Think of yourself as this small fruit, but also remember the ripe fruit. When troubles come that could make you fall from God, remember the saints in heaven who have survived persecution. God, who helped them in Jesus Christ, also helps you.

The Impossible Becomes Possible

The Word

"He will wipe away all tears from their eyes. There will be no more death, no more grief, crying, or pain. The old things have disappeared." Then the One who sits on the throne said, "And now I make all things new!" Revelation 21:4-5a (From the Epistle for the Fifth Sunday of Easter)

The World

Two identical paper sacks and a dozen marbles. Wad up one sack and tear several holes in it — including holes at the bottom of the sack.

Listen to this promise: "There will be no more death, no more grief, crying, or pain." Doesn't that sound great? Imagine what life would be like if we had no pain, sorrow, or death. Watch a news program or read a newspaper and leave out all the things about pain, sorrow, and death. You won't have much left. We spend a lot of our time worrying about or working against pain, sorrow, and death.

But our Bible reading promises that all grief will be gone. That sounds impossible. To see how impossible it is, look at this sack (the messed up one). When I put marbles in it, they fall out. (Do it.) If you used this sack to carry the marbles to school, you'd lose all the marbles before you got there.

Now suppose I promise: "This sack will hold all your marbles. You won't lose a single one." Sounds impossible. But sometimes there is a possible way to do impossible things. Look: (Take all the marbles out of the sack. Put the messed up sack inside the good sack. Now put the marbles inside the messed up sack.) See, the marbles will not fall out. They won't get lost. The promise is true.

And the promise that we will have no more pain, sorrow, or death is also true. Our Bible reading not only gives us the promise but it also tells us how God will keep the promise. Listen: "The old things have disappeared. . . . And now I make all things new!" Remember how the old sack disappeared when I put it in the new one? Now the new sack holds the marbles.

Our lives are the same. We are like this old sack. The holes in our lives are caused by sin. We have suffering, pain, and sorrow while we are on earth; and the time will come when we will die.

But Christ is like this new sack. He lived without sin; so there are no holes in His life. He went through death and rose again without being destroyed. Now He invites us to put our lives inside His life. Our old life disappears. His new life becomes a part of us.

We will have pains and sorrows on earth. We still see people die. We will die sometime. But we have the promise that all pain, sorrow, and death will be gone in heaven. Then we will live with Christ. Our old life will disappear. We will be a part of His new life.

Notice What Is Missing

The Word

I did not see a temple in the city, because its temple is the Lord God, the Almighty, and the Lamb. The city has no need of the sun or the moon to shine on it, because the glory of God shines on it, and the Lamb is its lamp. Revelation 21:22-23 (From the Epistle for the Sixth Sunday of Easter)

The World

Two scenes: One a city with a church; the other the same picture without the church. (Scenes may be skyline drawings on large posters or on transparencies for an overhead projector.)

Have you ever played the game where you look at two pictures and try to find the difference between the two? Let's try it. Look at these two pictures. First this one (with church). Now this one (without the church). Did you see the difference? That was easy—the church is missing from this one.

St. John noticed something like this in our Bible reading for today. God gave the apostle a vision of heaven. St. John had a difficult time describing heaven for us, because it is beyond our human understanding. But listen to one thing he did say, "I did not see a temple in the city, because its temple is the Lord God, the Almighty, and the Lamb."

John noticed that there is no church building in heaven. We might think that heaven would have the biggest and the best church buildings we had ever seen. But, no, he says there is no temple.

The temple was important in Jerusalem. Until Christ came, people took animals to the altar in the temple to sacrifice them. The sacrifices reminded the people that they needed a Savior to pay for their sin.

Now we have church buildings rather than temples. But we

still have an altar. The altar reminds us that Christ came to be our sacrifice. We don't have to bring animals. Instead we come before the altar to hear the story of Christ. We see Him as the Lamb of God who was offered to pay for the sins of the world. We gather together before the altar to share with one another the love Christ has given to all people.

But in heaven we will not have a temple, a church building, or that kind of altar. And John tells us why. He writes: "It's temple is the Lord God, the Almighty, and the Lamb." Instead of having a reminder about the Savior, we will be with the Savior Himself. There is no temple or church in heaven because Christ is present with all who are there.

St. John tells us this to remind us that on earth we still need the message of the altar. We need to receive the blessings of grace and forgiveness that Christ gave us when He died for us. We need to give gifts at the altar to grow in our love for God.

But always remember that the altar is a reminder. It is a string around your finger to tell you that you are going to heaven where you will be with the Christ you now worship.

When You Know You'll Pass the Test

The Word

"Listen!" says Jesus. "I am coming soon! I will bring My rewards with Me to give to each one according to what he has done. I am the Alpha and the Omega, the first and the last, the beginning and the end." Revelation 22:12-13 (From the Epistle for the Seventh Sunday of Easter)

The World

A sign with large letters that says, "You must be this tall to go on this ride," with an arrow to indicate height; tape; and a child.

Almost everyone likes to go to amusement parks (or name a nearby attraction such as Six Flags). But some of the rides are not for small children. The rides that could be dangerous have signs like this. (Tape the sign to a wall or piece of furniture so it will not exclude the child you plan to use.) Every person who wants to go on that ride must be at least this high (point to the arrow).

Jennifer, would you come up and see if you pass the test. Stand beside the arrow. Yes, you are tall enough. You can go on this ride. But it is a large park, and there are other rides. Suppose you want to ride on the roller coaster very much. But you don't know if you can pass the test. What if the arrow is higher at the roller coaster. But when you find the ride that you want, you discover that it has the exact same sign as the first. We don't have to measure you again. We know you pass; because it's the same sign. You have no worries. You passed the first test; so you know you'll pass the last one.

This idea of the same test being both first and last can help us understand our lives as Christians. The first test was when we came to know Christ. And He passed it for us. He didn't tell us to save ourselves. Instead, He came to save us. When we came to the first test, Jesus said, "Don't worry. I'll pass the test for you."

As we live as Christians, we sometimes wonder if we will have to pass other tests. And we wonder if the test will be more difficult. We especially think about the last test on Judgment Day. Our Bible reading tells us what Jesus will say on that day. It says, "'Listen!' says Jesus, 'I am coming soon! I will bring My rewards with Me to give to each one according to what he has done. I am the Alpha and the Omega, the first and the last, the beginning and the end.'"

Jesus is both the first and the last test. He is both Alpha, that is, A, and Omega, that is, Z. The first test was a test of grace—Jesus passed it for us. The last test will be a test of grace—Jesus will pass that for us too. Because Christ is both first and last, we know that on Judgment Day we will be judged by the same kind and loving Savior who gave His life for us long ago.

During our lives here we are somewhere between the first and last, between A and Z. We know Christ came first and called us to be with Him. We know He will be there at the last to keep us with Him forever. Also remember that He is with us now. Today also, we live with the love and grace of Christ.

When the Spirit Is Poured, Things Happen

The Word

This is what I will do in the last days, God says: I will pour out My Spirit upon all men. Your sons and your daughters will prophesy; your young men will see visions; and your old men will dream dreams. . . . And then, whoever calls on the name of the Lord will be saved. Acts 2:17, 21 (From the Epistle for Pentecost)

The World

A pitcher of water, a water glass, a kitchen pan, a large bowl.

Our Bible reading has a beautiful way of telling us how the Holy Spirit will come to us. God says, "I will pour out My Spirit on all people." The word pouring sounds generous. And that's the way God is with the Holy Spirit. The Spirit has many blessings for our lives. He often gives us so much more than we use.

The Holy Spirit is poured on us in different ways. The Bible reading says that some will prophesy, others will see visions, others will dream dreams. In other parts of the Bible we can read about many more gifts that the Holy Spirit pours into our lives.

This pitcher has water. I can pour the water into the glass—then it is for drinking. I can pour it into this pan, over some vegetables—then it is for cooking. I can pour the water into this bowl—then it could be used to wash fresh vegetables. The same water can be poured for many different uses.

The Holy Spirit is also poured upon us for many different purposes. We need to know that the power of the Spirit is given to us all. We are baptized in the name of the Holy Spirit. We receive His power. Even though we have the power in different ways, it all comes from the same Spirit.

Even though we receive different ways to use the power of the

Spirit, the Spirit does not divide us. Instead the Spirit unites us. When we receive a gift from the Spirit, we receive it not just for our own use but to share with others. When others receive a gift that we do not have, we are to share the joy and benefit of our gift with them.

The Holy Spirit unites us because He calls all of us to believe in Jesus Christ. After telling us all the different blessings that come from the outpouring of the Spirit, our Bible reading says, "And then, whoever calls on the name of the Lord will be saved."

The Holy Spirit has called us to believe in Christ as our Savior. Just as we do not earn our salvation by being good, because Christ was good in our place; we also do not earn our salvation by believing in Him. Even our faith is a gift of God through the power of the Spirit.

And because we have faith in Christ by the Spirit's power, we can also serve God by the Spirit's power. And our serving God by the power of the Spirit leads others to call upon Christ as their Savior.

Find Good on the Bad Side

The Word

He has brought us, by faith, into this experience of God's grace in which we now live. We rejoice, then, in the hope we have of sharing God's glory! And we also rejoice in our troubles, because we know that trouble produces endurance, endurance brings God's approval, and His approval creates hope. Romans 5:2-4. (From the Epistle for the First Sunday After Pentecost)

The World

A large piece of paper with an orderly pattern of lines drawn on one side and a jumble of mixed-up lines on the other.

The first part of our Bible reading is easy to understand. It says that because Christ has made us right with God, we have many good things in our lives. And we are happy about it.

Because Christ has made us right with God, our lives can be like this (paper with orderly pattern). Christ has made the parts of our lives fit together in a neat pattern. Because of Christ our sins are forgiven; so our mistakes don't show. Because of Christ we can get along with one another in our families and school, just as these lines work together to make a pattern. Because of Christ we know God is with us now and that we will go to heaven, just as these lines make a pattern, so you could know what the next one would be even without seeing it.

But we must also admit that there is another side of our lives. (Turn the paper over.) Our lives are also big messes. Even though we are saved, we are still sinners. Even though we are going to heaven, we still live in a world of trouble and sorrow. Parts of our lives are all mixed up.

But notice what our Bible reading says: "We rejoice in our troubles, because we know that trouble produces endurance,

endurance brings God's approval, and His approval creates hope."

We don't have to pretend that everything in our lives is great. (Hold the paper close to yourself with the orderly side showing.) We don't have to hide the fact that we have problems—and that we've caused many of the problems ourselves.

God created our lives to be like this (orderly side), but when we made a mess (reverse paper) God did not destroy us. If He would have destroyed the bad side of our lives, He would also have destroyed the good side. If He would have cut out part of the bad side, He would also have cut out part of the good. Instead God sent Christ to be on this side (messed-up side) with us. The Holy Spirit also comes to us to help us even in our problems.

Because God is with us on this side, we can find blessings even in our problems. It does not mean that the wrong things we do are good. But it means that God is good, and He will help us even when we are wrong. And when we receive His help, we become stronger. We grow in faith when we know God is with us in our problems and that He forgives our sins. We become stronger Christians when we have to pray and depend totally on God, and He helps us.

Always see the good in your life and be happy about it. But also look for good on the bad side. See how God has helped you and know that He will always continue to help you.

Keep the Right Key

The Word

I am surprised at you! In no time at all you are deserting the one who called you by the grace of Christ and are going to another gospel. Actually, there is no "other gospel," but I say this because there are some people who are upsetting you and trying to change the Gospel of Christ. Galatians 1:6-7 (From the Epistle for the Second Sunday After Pentecost)

The World

A box of keys, including the key to the building you are in.

Suppose you left a library book in church after the service today. The book is due on Monday, so you would come back this afternoon to get it. But the door would be locked. You couldn't get in unless someone gave you this key. With the key you could open the door and get your book.

Then you might take the key home and throw it in a box of keys. Later, if you needed to get in the church, you might grab a key from the box. But this key won't open the door. Nor will this one. Only the right key will open the door. The other keys are good keys, but they are good for other locks. You need one special key for the church door.

In our Bible reading St. Paul tells us that the Gospel is like a key. We want to get into heaven. God gave us the way when He sent His Son to be our Savior. Christ opened the door to heaven for us. The Gospel, which is the good news about Christ, is our key.

But then listen to what the Bible reading says, "I am surprised at you! In no time at all you are deserting the one who called you by the grace of Christ, and are going to another gospel. Actually, there is no 'other gospel,' but I say this because there are some people who are upsetting you and trying to change the Gospel of Christ."

The Gospel is the good news that we are saved. There can be other kinds of good news. School is over and you are promoted to another grade. Your favorite team won a ball game. You are going on vacation. Those things are good news like these (other keys in the box) are all good keys. But just as only one key opens the door to this building, only one kind of good news opens the door to heaven—and that is the good news that Christ is your Savior. Enjoy all the other good news in your life, but do not depend on anything else to save you.

You might say that you got this key to open the door when you wanted to get your book. Then you could ask what key you would use if you wanted to put flowers on the altar. And what key would you use if you wanted to practice on the organ? Or what key would you use if you were to clean the church? Of course, the answer is always the same. This key opens the door.

So also the Gospel is the key to heaven, but it is also the key to be with Christ here on earth. If Christ loves us so much that He died in our place so we can be in heaven, He also loves us enough to be with us now. When we need help on earth, let's not look for other keys. Instead, use the key of the Gospel.

When you are sad and lonely, do not look for another key to solve your problem, but use the key Christ has given you. Remember His love for you. When you are angry, let Christ be the key that removes the anger. When you are tempted, let Christ be the key that helps you with that temptation.

Paul was surprised that people who had the Gospel that worked would leave it for other gospels that would not work. Learn to use the real Gospel; then you won't want any other.

Who Made Your Gospel?

The Word

Let me tell you this, my brothers, that the Gospel I preach was not made by man. I did not receive it from any man, nor did anyone teach it to me. Instead, it was Jesus Christ Himself who revealed it to me. Galatians 1:11-12 (From the Epistle for the Third Sunday After Pentecost)

The World

A dollar bill and a piece of paper play money.

Suppose you wanted to buy an ice cream cone. You might take this dollar and go to a store that sold ice cream. You'd pay for the cone and enjoy it. Simple, right?

But suppose that you gave the clerk this (the play money)? You wouldn't get the ice cream. In one sense you can call this a dollar. If you were playing a game, you might give it to another player and say, "Here is a dollar." But that's part of a game. It's pretend. Buying the ice cream cone is not a game. If you want real ice cream, you need real money.

In our Bible reading St. Paul warns us against having a pretend gospel. "The Gospel I preach was not made by man," he says, "I did not receive it from any man, nor did anyone teach it to me. Instead, it was Jesus Christ Himself who revealed it to me." The real Gospel is the good news that Christ died for us and rose again. His death paid for our sins. Since we have real sins, we need a real payment—not pretend. He rose from the dead to give us a new life. If we want a real eternal life, not a pretend one, we need a real resurrection.

But just as we can make play money, we can also make a play gospel. One pretend gospel is this: If you are good and do the best you can, you will go to heaven. That says you have to save yourself. People who believe that pretend gospel comfort each other when someone dies by saying, "He was such a good person"; then they tell about all the good things the dead person did.

But that is a pretend gospel. The real Gospel says we are saved not because we are good but because Christ was good for us.

Another pretend gospel is said this way: "If God is good, He won't let anyone go to hell. I can't imagine God wanting anyone to suffer; so He'll take care of us all."

True, God tells us that He does not want anyone to go to hell. And God gave a way for all people to be saved through Jesus. But His way is not to ignore our sins. His way is to pay for our sins. It is a pretend gospel to say that God will just forget about our evil.

Another pretend gospel is the idea that there is no heaven or hell. As long as we think there is no life after death, we can also think we don't need a Savior. But God did not make us to be throw away people. He made us to live forever. And He gave us a way to have eternal life through Christ.

You can think of other pretend gospels. To check if the message you hear is real ask yourself: Who made it? The difference between the real and pretend money is in who made it and why it was made. The same is true about messages that tell us about eternal life. When people make up their own gospels, they always have to depend upon themselves. When God gives us His Gospel, He let's us depend on Him.

A New Way to Live

The Word

So far as the Law is concerned, however, I am dead — killed by the Law itself — in order that I might live for God. I have been put to death with Christ on His cross, so that it is no longer I who live, but it is Christ who lives in me. This life that I live now, I live by faith in the Son of God, who loved me and gave His life for me. Galatians 2:19-20. (From the Epistle for the Fourth Sunday After Pentecost)

The World

Two balloons (different colors) and a scissors.

A balloon is made to be used like this: (Blow up one balloon). If it can't be blown up, a balloon might as well be thrown away. (Let the air out and cut off the closed end of the balloon.) Now the balloon is worthless.

In our Bible reading Paul says that he is worthless—even worse, he says he is dead. He writes, "So far as the Law is concerned, however, I am dead—killed by the Law itself." God's Law says we must be perfect as God is perfect. But Paul knew that he was not perfect. He had sinned and sin causes death. So he was like this balloon. He could no longer serve his purpose in life. By the Law he was dead.

But Paul doesn't say that his life is ended. Instead, he adds, "I have been put to death with Christ on his cross, so that it is no longer I who live, but it is Christ who lives in me." Rather than just die because of sin, Paul claims to have found a special way to die—with Christ on the cross. And remember that after Christ died on the cross He came back to life. Paul therefore claims that since Christ died for him on the cross, Christ also lives for him. When Paul said he was dead, he added, "so far as the Law is concerned." But according to the Gospel Paul is very much alive. He has a new life in Christ.

Back to the balloons. Instead of throwing this balloon away, we can put a new life in it too. See: (Put the other balloon inside the cut balloon by inserting it through the cut end first. Then poke the mouth of the good balloon out through the mouth of the cut balloon. Blow up the good balloon so it will also expand the cut balloon. Practice ahead of time to determine if you have enough air pressure to do it. If you smoke, you may need a nonsmoker to help.)

See: The balloon that could not be blown up by itself is again filled with air. The good balloon inside makes the broken balloon usable again. Christ in us also makes us whole again. Because Christ has no sin He can give us His holiness by living in us.

When you feel the problem of sin and, like Paul, realize that sin causes your death; remember these two balloons. When you feel guilty and worthless, remember that Christ has come into your life and that He removes your guilt and gives you a new life. When you think you cannot forgive someone, or help someone, or love someone; remember how Christ comes into your life and gives you a new life. By His power you can forgive others. You can help others. You can love others.

We Are One in Jesus Christ

The Word

You were baptized into union with Christ, and so have taken upon yourselves the qualities of Christ Himself. So there is no difference between Jews and Gentiles, between slaves and free men, between men and women: you are all one in union with Christ Jesus. Galatians 3:27-28 (From the Epistle for the Fifth Sunday After Pentecost)

The World

Glass jars, each containing an ingredient for bread (flour, sugar, milk, shortening, yeast), and a loaf of bread.

What if I were to tell you that each of these jars contained the same thing? Would you believe that there is no difference in the contents of the jars? I doubt it. You can see the difference between some. This one (milk) is a liquid and others are not. These two (sugar and flour) might look alike at a distance, but up close you can see that one is finer than the other. And if you tasted them you would know that one is sugar and the other flour.

But now listen to what our Bible reading says: "So there is no difference between Jews and Gentiles, between slaves and free men, between men and women." That's hard to believe too. You could see the differences between Jews and Gentiles. They were different races. They wore different clothes and spoke different languages. And certainly the differences between slaves and free people were obvious. Even in our day when we stress the fact that men and women are equal, we do not say there are no differences between men and women. But St. Paul did.

But before we decide that St. Paul was wrong, let's listen to the reason that he thinks there are no differences among us: "You were baptized into union with Christ, and so have taken upon yourselves the qualities of Christ Himself."

Sure, there are differences between people. But when we are baptized into Christ, something happens to us. Christ becomes a part of us—of each of us. Therefore we are all alike as baptized children of God. Look back at these jars. Each contains something different. But if all of these things were mixed together and baked, we would have this (bread). You can see and taste the difference between the separate ingredients of bread, but after the bread is baked they all become one in a loaf. Something has happened to each ingredient.

And something happens to us when we become Christians. We are changed. Our sins are forgiven. We have a new life. We are connected to Christ and through Him we are also connected with one another. As individuals we are still different. Each of you has something special and different about you. But as Christians we are all united. Paul was right: there is no difference.

When you see other people, remember that Christ loves them too. Perhaps He has by His gift of life changed them as He has changed you. If so, you belong together.

Who Steers Your Life?

The Word

What I say is this: let the Spirit direct your lives, and do not satisfy the desires of the human nature. For what our human nature wants is opposed to what the Spirit wants, and what the Spirit wants is opposed to what human nature wants. The two are enemies, and this means that you cannot do what you want to do. Galatians 5:16-17 (From the Epistle for the Sixth Sunday After Pentecost)

The World

A toy car or other toy that has a wheel which may be turned (or a toy that has a wheel that can be removed). A flat surface on which to run the toy.

Suppose your life was one long trip in a car like this. You are born here (one end of the flat surface) and you want to be over there (other end) when you die. That should be an easy trip—like this. (Push the car from one end of surface to the other.)

But life isn't that simple. If this car represents your life, then sin would mean that the wheels were turned the wrong way (or one wheel was missing). When the wheels are turned look what happens. (Start at the same place but go off the side.) Sin takes your life off course. Sin makes you go in the wrong direction. Sin keeps you from going where you should go.

Our Bible reading tells you to watch out when sin guides your life. It says: "Let the Spirit direct your lives, and do not satisfy the desires of the human nature. For what our human nature wants is oppossed to what the Spirit wants, and what the Spirit wants is oppossed to what human nature wants. The two are enemies, and this means that you cannot do what you want to do."

Just as sin wants to turn the wheel of your life to make you go off the side, the Holy Spirit tries to straighten the wheels out so you can get to the other end. You can imagine what life is like with two forces trying to control the driving. One always tries to run off on either side. The other tries to keep the car on the road. The Bible reading said that the Spirit in us works against our human nature and the human nature works against the Spirit.

Let's think of some examples. (Place car on the surface.) Our human natures wants us to lie or cheat if we feel we will gain something from it. But that turns the wheel off the road. One of the problems of our human nature is that we only look at the present and decide what is best just for now. Our human nature will make us say rude and hurtful things even to people we love. We will be selfish and not help others. Each time such things happen our lives are turned off course.

But the Holy Spirit does not want our lives to be destroyed. God loves us. He wants us to reach the other end to be with Him. So the Spirit tells us when we turn the wrong way. He tells us we are forgiven because Christ is our Savior. He turns us back in the right direction.

The Bible reading reminds us we cannot always control our lives. It says, "You cannot do what you want to do." But you can know when you are being pulled to do wrong and you can use the Spirit's power to get back on course.

When the Other Person Is Wrong

The Word

My brothers, if someone is caught in any kind of wrongdoing, those of you who are spiritual should set him right; but you must do it in a gentle way. And keep an eye on yourself, so that you will not be tempted too. Help carry one another's burdens, and in this way you will obey the law of Christ. Galatians 6:1-2 (From the Epistle for the Seventh Sunday After Pentecost)

The World

A clean plate, a bottle of catsup, a paper towel.

Our Bible reading today tells us what to do when we notice that someone else is doing something wrong. So let's have an example of a wrong. This is a clean plate—the way it should be before a meal. But suppose while preparing the dinner someone dropped a glob of catsup on the plate. (Do it.) That mess on the plate will represent something wrong.

What will you do about it? You could point at it and say, "Hey, look, everyone, see the mess on the plate." To make sure everyone saw the mess you might put your finger in it and spread it around. But now the mess on the plate is worse. And you have the same mess on your finger.

Instead, let's listen to what the Bible reading tells us. It says, "If someone is caught in any kind of wrongdoing, those of you who are spiritual should set him right; but you must do it in a gentle way. Keep your eye on yourself, so that you will not be tempted also."

Notice that I did two things wrong when I saw the glob on the plate. In the first place I got it on myself. By showing someone else's mess I became a mess too. The Bible warns us not to be tempted to follow another person's sin. Don't hate a person because he hates others. Don't lie about a person who lies. Your sin may not be the same as another's, but it is still sin. If someone else does wrong and you say bad things and cause them more problems, you also are wrong. You'd be like me when I got the mess on my finger.

The Bible reading also says we must show another person's fault in a way that will help that person. When I pointed to the glob on the plate, I spread it around and made it worse. If you try to correct someone and you make the problem worse, you have done more harm than good.

Our reading also tells us what we should do. It says we are to help carry one another's burdens and follow the will of Christ. Instead of seeing other people's sins as something to find fault with, see the sins as a burden. Then you can help. If you are a spiritual person—that is one who has the new life in Christ—you can help a person who has done wrong.

See: (Take a paper towel and clean your finger; then wipe off the plate). I had a way to clean the mess off my finger. I used this towel. The towel is an example of Christ. He forgives our sins. He makes us clean. Because I have the towel to clean my hand, I can also clean the plate. Because I know Christ as my Savior, I can help another person be forgiven too.

As a Christian you must help others who do wrong. But always help in a way that brings the other person nearer to Christ. And stay close to Christ yourself.

Know What to Sort Out

The Word

When the true message, the Good News, first came to you, you heard of the hope it offers. So your faith and love are based on what you hope for, which is kept safe for you in heaven. Colossians 1:5 (From the Epistle for the Eighth Sunday After Pentecost)

The World

A stack of mail including an advertisement, magazine, bill, postcard, and letter.

Suppose this is the mail that was delivered to your home yesterday. As you look at the stack of mail, you would wonder if any of it is for you. Let's see—this is a bill. You don't want that. The letter is not for you. It is addressed to your mother and doesn't look interesting. Probably from an aunt or cousin or something. This is an advertisement for sheets and pillow cases. You don't want any. Well, that leaves the magazine. It looks kind of interesting. You might as well read it.

If you read the magazine and like it, you would probably think the mail was worthwhile. But if it was dull, you'd have to forget about the mail and find something else to do.

But before you leave you had better look through this stack one more time. Look! Here is a postcard—addressed to you. It is an invitation for you to spend a week at a camp with all the expenses paid. Wow! Isn't that great! Just think—if you had thought the mail was dull and hadn't found this, you would have missed the invitation. Or if you liked the magazine and hadn't looked for something else, you would have enjoyed the mail, but you would have missed the most important part.

Now let's apply the lesson of the stack of mail to our worship. Being in church offers a stack of things to do. Here you can see your friends, hear music, listen to a sermon, sing some, say a few prayers. You might think that none of those things are for you— or that none of it interests you. Or you might like one part and forget the rest. You might like seeing your friends, or the music, and pass the rest by.

But wait a minute. Just like in the mail, there is something special for you. It is a message that God loves you and has sent Jesus to be your Friend and Savior.

Some things about church may not be exciting to you. You may think that part of it is only for other people. And you may be right. But the message of Christ's love and forgiveness is for you.

The Christians in Colossae understood the message of Christ that had been preached to them. St. Paul wrote: "When the true message, the Good News, first came to you, you heard of the hope it offers. So your faith and love are based on what you hope for, which is kept safe for you in heaven." They recognized that the story of Christ changed their lives. They sorted through all the messages they received and found the hope of Christ. And they held on to it.

You can do the same. Too often adults will say they went to church for many years before they found the joy of knowing Christ. They didn't sort through all the things going on to find the hope that Christ gives to us all. Don't let that happen to you. Listen to Christ today. He wants to give you hope.

The Secret Is in You

The Word

God's plan is this: to make known His secret to His people, this rich and glorious secret which He has for all peoples. And the secret is this: Christ is in you, which means that you will share the glory of God. Colossians 1:27 (From the Epistle for the Ninth Sunday After Pentecost)

The World

An envelope with "Wednesday" written on the inside in large letters. Also in the envelope, a piece of paper that says, "Barbara's house" and another that says, "7:30." Another envelope with the words "for me" written on the inside. This envelope also contains a paper with the words "Christ died" and another that says, "Christ arose."

Our Bible reading tells us that God has a secret. It also says that He wants us to know the secret because it is for all people. So let's talk about secrets and how we share them with one another.

Suppose we are having a surprise party. If it is to be a surprise it must be a secret. So I will give you this invitation. The secret is in the envelope. Later you open it and you read, "Barbara's house." Now you know where the party will be. Then you read, "7:30." Now you know what time it will be. But look—the envelope is empty. You still don't know what day the party will be. You know where and what time but not the date. Yet I said the entire secret was in this envelope. Let's look again. The envelope is empty—but look: (tear the envelope open) The party is on Wednesday. The entire secret was in the envelope. Some of it was on the pieces of paper, but an important part was written on the envelope itself.

God's secret is not delivered in an envelope—instead, He shares His secret through people. He has told us who know the secret to tell others the good news that Jesus is the Savior of the world. We are like this envelope (open second envelope). We have the secret. See—the secret is this: "Christ died." Part of the secret is that God sent His Son to pay for sin. But that's not all. Listen: "Christ arose." The same One who died won a victory over death. He came back to life again. That seems like all of the secret. Christ died and arose again. The envelope is empty.

But look—there is more. (Tear open the envelope.) It says, "for me." Christ died for me. He arose again for me. When I share this secret with you, I not only tell you what God did in Christ but that He did it for me. And that He did it for you.

We are like this envelope. We know the story of Christ, and we can tell others how He died and rose again. But we have also become a part of the message. Our Bible reading says: "And the secret is this: Christ is in you, which means that you will share the glory of God."

Christ shares His love and forgiveness through you. He shares His life through you. That means the secret is not just something in you like the pieces of paper in the envelope. The secret is a part of you. Love and forgiveness in Christ are written on your life. You can share the secret with others.

Where Are You Getting Your Power?

The Word

Since you have accepted Christ Jesus as Lord, live in union with Him. Keep your roots deep in Him.... See to it, then, that no one makes a captive of you with the worthless deceit of human wisdom, which comes from the teachings handed down by men, and from the ruling spirits of the universe, and not from Christ....For when you were baptized, you were buried with Christ, and in Baptism you were also raised with Christ through your faith in the active power of God, who raised Him from death. Colossians 2:6-7a, 8, 12 (From the Epistle for the Tenth Sunday After Pentecost)

The World

A white paper napkin folded so it is about an inch wide. Two glasses of water, one colored red with food coloring and the other blue.

Our Bible reading reminds us of the blessings we have because we are baptized into Christ. It says, "For when you were baptized, you were buried with Christ, and in Baptism you were also raised with Christ through your faith in the active power of God, who raised Him from death." Notice it says you have already been buried and you have already been raised, because Christ did these things for you.

Let's use this water—it's colored red so you can see it—to show your baptism. This napkin is you. (Put one end of the napkin into the water.) See how your baptism changes you. It takes what is in Christ and puts it into you. Christ's love becomes your love. Christ's death becomes your death. Christ's life becomes your life. His power enters you.

That's why the Bible reading also tells us to stay in union with Christ. St. Paul says to keep our roots deep in Him. Even though you were baptized a long time ago, you are still baptized today. As long as you stay with Christ, you continue to receive the power He offers.

But our Bible reading also warns us about other powers in our lives. It says, "See to it, then, that no one makes a captive of you with the worthless deceit of human wisdom, which comes from the teachings handed down by men, and from the ruling spirits of the universe, and not from Christ."

Just as we receive power from Christ in our baptism, we can receive evil power from the world. We will let this blue water represent the evil power that Paul warned us against. (Dip the other end of the napkin into the blue water.) This shows us how we live. From Christ we receive power to live a good life. But from the world we receive power to do wrong. (Move the napkin back and forth between the two glasses.)

We often feel that many people are telling us what to do. Parents, teachers, friends, TV ads, songs—all tell us what to do or make us want to do things. But think about the way others tell you what to do. Which power do they ask you to use? Are they asking you to stay rooted with Christ? Are they urging you to use the new life you received in Baptism? Or do others try to get you to do wrong? Do they encourage that part of your life that wants to lie, be selfish, or hurt others?

Then remember your baptism and the new life you have in Christ. Use it.

Move from the Old to the New

The Word

You have been raised to life with Christ. Set your hearts, then, on the things that are in heaven, where Christ sits on His throne at the right side of God.... You must put to death, then, the earthly desires at work in you, such as immorality, indecency, lust, evil passions, and greed (for greediness is a form of idol worship). Colossians 3:1, 5 (From the Epistle for the Eleventh Sunday After Pentecost)

The World

Pictures (from a magazine or simple outline sketches) of an old, rundown house and a new, attractive house. A change of address card from the Post Office.

A family lived in this old, rundown house. The roof leaked, the plumbing didn't work. Rats lived in the basement. This house was a bad place to live.

But someone built the family a beautiful, new home like this. The house was large, clean, and comfortable. The family said they appreciated the new house. They had dinner in the new home, but at bedtime they went back to the old house. The next day they visited the new house—sometimes they would even sleep there. But they kept going back to the old home. The mailman left this change of address card for them. The card shows when a family moves from an old address to a new address. But they never used the card. They liked the new house, but they kept the old house as their permanent address.

That sounds like a strange story. All of us would prefer the new house. But we might be doing the same thing—in a different way. By ourselves we are sinful people, and our lives are like the old house. But Christ gave us a new life—a life that looks like this new house. Instead of living in the old way of sin, Jesus gave us a new way to live in joy and goodness.

But have we sent in our change of address card? Are we willing to give up the old way of living to move into the new life?

Our Bible reading tells us about the old life and the new life. It says, "You have been raised to life with Christ. Set your hearts, then, on the things that are in heaven, where Christ sits on His throne at the right side of God. . . . You must put to death, then, the earthly desires at work in you, such as immorality, indecency, lust, evil passions, and greed (for greediness is a form of idol worship)."

If we are going to move into the new life with Christ, we must move out of the old life of sin. We must throw out the evil things that hurt us and others. We must move into the new life that helps us and others.

Because we are sinners we will remember the ways of the old life as long as we live on this earth. And when we sin, it is as though we are going back to the old house. But we can fight against sin, because Christ has given us this new life. He has signed our change of address card that says we live with Him now and that we will be with Him forever.

Don't Limit Your Faith

The Word

To have faith is to be sure of the things we hope for, to be certain of the things we cannot see. Hebrews 11:1 (From the Epistle for the Twelfth Sunday After Pentecost)

The World

A sack of ripe peaches (or other fruit in season) and a small basket.

Suppose you visited a family that had a large peach orchard, and the trees were filled with ripe fruit. See how beautiful a ripe peach is! I have only a sackful here. Imagine what a whole orchard of ripe peaches would look like. Imagine the delicious smell!

If the person who owned the orchard were a friend, he might tell you that you could have all the peaches you wanted. But the only container you have is this one, small basket. It won't hold many peaches. See? (Fill the basket.) Then your friend might say, "I wanted you to have more than that. I'll tell you what I'll do. If you want, you may take that small basket today. Or, if you wait until tomorrow, I'll bring you a whole bushel basket of peaches."

Now you have a choice. This small basket right now or a much larger basket tomorrow. You might think, "If I take the small basket now, I'll be sure of having at least some. My friend might forget or be too busy to bring me the big basket tomorrow."

Your final decision would show how much you trusted your friend. If you knew that he would do what he said, you could wait for the big basket. Otherwise you would take the little basket now.

Let's use the idea of the peaches and the basket to help us understand why God asks us to live by faith. Our Bible reading says, "To have faith is to be sure of the things we hope for, to be certain of the things we cannot see." We sometimes wonder why God expects us to live by faith. Why doesn't He show us proof, so we could see for ourselves? If only we had one glimpse of heaven. Or if we saw Jesus in person just one time. You can add to the list of things that God could do to remove doubts from our minds.

However, all the great mysteries of God are like that orchard of peaches. And our minds are like this little basket. We cannot understand everything about God. Our minds are too limited. We can talk about heaven, but it is more than we can describe. We know that God became a person in Jesus and that He died and rose again, but how that happened is beyond our ability to understand.

So God says, "Don't limit My gifts to those you can understand. Trust Me. Live by faith in Me, and I will give you much more than you can even dream of now."

Are you willing to live by faith—to trust that what Christ has done does change your life? Are you willing to go beyond your understanding and believe there is an eternal home for you in heaven? Or will you say, "No, I won't wait for what you might give me later. I want only what I can see and understand now."

Our Bible reading tells us that faith makes us sure of the things we hope for. It tells us we can be certain even of things we have not seen. We can be sure, because the promise comes from God.

The Way Back to the Right Track

The Word

Let us keep our eyes fixed on Jesus, on whom our faith depends from beginning to end.... Endure what you suffer as being a father's punishment; because your suffering shows that God is treating you as His sons. Hebrews 12:2a, 7a (From the Epistle for the Thirteenth Sunday After Pentecost)

The World

A game board (as shown) on a large poster that can be folded. A piece of paper with tape to be used as a marker.

Often you have to decide what you will say and what you will do. Our Bible reading for today helps you make decisions. And it will also help you when you make the wrong decision.

We'll use this game as an illustration. (Show the game with the right side folded so only 3 spaces after the "Y" can be seen.) This marker is you, and you are here (2 spaces before the "Y"). It's your turn, and you roll a 5. But as you move, you have to make a choice. Since you can't see the end of the game, you have to decide which way looks the best. This way has a cross—remember that stands for suffering and death. This way has a happy face. So you move this way. (Place marker on the happy face.)

But (open the game board) you made the wrong choice. This way leads to a dead end. If you refuse to admit you were wrong, you could keep moving forward. You do that in life if you lie, then keep on lying; if you hate, then keep on hating; if you ignore God, then keep on ignoring God. That way you punish yourself. Because we are sinners, we all make wrong choices. But because we have a Savior, we do not need to continue to follow wrong with more wrong.

Our Bible reading offers us help. It says, "Endure what you

97

suffer as being a father's punishment; because your suffering shows that God is treating you as His sons." When you have discovered you are wrong (move marker back to happy face), you can turn around and start over.

Starting over may be punishment, but it is punishment that helps rather than hurts. God turns us around, because He loves us and does not want us to continue to hurt ourselves by going the wrong way.

The Bible reading also tells us why God's punishment can help us. It says, "Let us keep our eyes fixed on Jesus, on whom our faith depends from beginning to end." When we do wrong, we can turn around and go back, because Jesus went the way of the cross for us. He took the punishment that would have destroyed us when He landed on this place (the cross) for us. Now when we land in the place of death and punishment, we are not destroyed. Instead, we can go on.

And look—see the happy faces here. This way can offer real happiness, because the cross is first. Our guilt is removed. We can live with God forever.

Daydream or for Real?

The Word

You have not come, as the people of Israel came, to what you can feel, to Mount Sinai with its blazing fire, the darkness and the gloom, the storm, the noise of a trumpet, and the sound of a voice.... Instead, you have come to Mount Zion and to the city of the living God, the heavenly Jerusalem, with its thousands of angels.... You have come to Jesus. Hebrews 12:18-19a, 22, 24a (From the Epistle for the Fourteenth Sunday After Pentecost)

The World

A sealed, addressed envelope with a return address.

We all like to have something to look forward to. For example, if you enter a contest that you read about in a magazine, you look forward to receiving mail each day. You can wonder whether or not you will win. You can even daydream about what you will do with the prize money. You can have fun as you plan what to do with all that money.

Then one day the letter arrives. Waiting for the mail is no longer a daydream. It is real. If you win the contest—your daydream comes true. But if you lose, you not only lose the contest, but you also lose the daydream. That almost makes you wish the letter had not arrived. But you have to face reality sometime.

We also look forward to being with God. We know that heaven must be a great place and that God must be the greatest. We can talk about how we want to "live in the house of the Lord forever." But is that real? Or is it just a daydream? What happens when you actually face God? Will you be glad? Or will you be like one who has gotten a letter that brings good or bad news? Would you rather keep the daydream?

Our Bible reading tells us about the people of Israel. They

always talked about being with God. They wanted to see God. But when they finally arrived at Mount Sinai, where God told them He would speak to them, they were afraid. When they came close to the presence of God, they decided they would rather keep their daydream than face reality. Could that happen to us?

The Bible reading tells us that we need not come before God in the same way the Israelites did. It says, "Instead, you have come to Mount Zion and to the city of the living God, the heavenly Jerusalem, with its thousands of angels. . . . You have come to Jesus."

The Israelites came before God carrying their sins. They came to hear the Law that condemned them. We would not want to face God that way either. We'd be better off having a daydream about a pleasant God than facing an angry God.

But remember: Before we go to God, God has come to us. He came to us as Jesus Christ, the Savior. He came to remove that load of sin by taking it on Himself. Now we can come to God with joy.

Jesus makes the daydream of being with God a reality. When you come face to face with God, either at your death or on Judgment Day, you need not have doubts about what will happen as you would if you received a letter about your entry in a contest. Christ has already won for you. Christ is with you now. You will be with Him forever. That is reality.

Good Is Better Than Evil

The Word

Ask God to bless those who persecute you; yes, ask Him to bless, not to curse.... If someone does evil to you, do not pay him back with evil. Try to do what all men consider to be good.... Do not let evil defeat you; instead, conquer evil with good. Romans 12:14, 17, 21 (From the Epistle for the Fifteenth Sunday After Pentecost)

The World

A flashlight and a red transparency (one from an overhead projector or make one with red cellophane or plastic).

All of us agree that good is better than evil. But often we think that good is better than evil only when we are talking about others. Good is better than evil when other people do not lie, steal, hate, curse, or do any of the other evil things that hurt others.

To see this evil let's imagine for now only that red is evil. You can see it (show transparency). When others talk to me through evil, they hurt me. (Shine the light through the transparency so red light lands on your face.) Words or deeds that are done through evil put evil on me. If people would speak good things and do good things to me (remove the transparency), I would be happier. Good is better than evil.

But we must also remember that good is better than evil when we speak and act. If someone says evil things to me (shine the light through the transparency so red light lands on your face), and I also speak evil to that person (shine the light from your side through the transparency on another), then I am sharing the same evil that the other person did to me.

The evil that I do is just as bad as the evil that others do. If I really agree that good is better than evil, then I should do good to others even though they do evil to me.

Listen to what our Bible reading says, "Ask God to bless those who persecute you; yes, ask Him to bless, not to curse. . . . If someone does evil to you, do not pay him back with evil. Try to do what all men consider to be good. . . . Do not let evil defeat you; instead, conquer evil with good."

That means if someone does evil to you (shine red light on self), you do not answer in the same way. Instead you return good (shine light directly on another person) to that person.

This is possible only because we know what Christ has done for us. He put Himself behind evil for us. (If available, shine the light through the transparency on a cross or symbol of Jesus.) He took our evil and gave us love, mercy, forgiveness and a new life. His good overcomes our evil.

The evil that destroys us is not the evil that others do to us. It is the evil that we do to others. Let Christ remove that evil.

I Command or I Request?

The Word

For this reason I could be bold enough, as your brother in Christ, to order you to do what should be done. But love compels me to make a request instead. Philemon 8-9a (From the Epistle for the Sixteenth Sunday After Pentecost)

The World

Three quarters, two dimes, and a nickel.

On a Saturday night a father gave his son an allowance for the week. Here it is—three quarters, two dimes, and a nickel—that's one dollar. Then the father said, "Remember you have to give 10 percent of your allowance to the church. That means you should give one of the dimes."

So the next morning the son put a dime in the offering plate.

Another father gave his son the same allowance—three quarters, two dimes, and a nickel. He said, "Remember to give some of your allowance to church."

The son asked, "How much do I have to give?"

"Don't give what you have to," said the father. "Give what you want to. Remember that God has given you all that you have and, because Christ is your Savior, all of your money is used to show your faith—not only that which you give, but also what you spend. And remember, the money you give helps share Jesus with others."

The second son also put one dime in the church offering.

Since both boys gave the same amount, we might think they gave the same thing. But they didn't. The first boy gave because he had to. The second gave because he wanted to.

Our Bible reading talks about these two ways of serving God. It says, "For this reason I could be bold enough, as your brother in Christ, to order you to do what should be done. But love compels me to make a request instead." Paul was sending a slave back to his owner, Philemon. Both Philemon and the slave had become Christians since the slave had run away. Paul told Philemon that he could order him to free the slave. But instead he trusts Philemon to follow Jesus. Paul asks him to free the slave.

When we read the Bible, we find both commands and requests from God. When we ignore God's love in Christ, we have to listen to the commands of God. But when we know Christ has freed us from sin, God can request us to follow Him and do His will. We then follow in love.

God wants us to obey Him because we love and respect Him. When we do, we are doing what God requests us to do. But if we are only afraid that God might punish us, then we will do only those things that He has commanded us to do.

Which do you need—God's command or God's request? Apply your answer not only to the way you give your money, but also to the way you obey your parents, behave at school, speak with your friends, and do your work.

Remember that everything God asks you to do is for your own good. He loves you and wants to protect you from evil. See His love in Christ, and do what He requests because you want to.

A Good Bad Example

The Word

This is a true saying, to be completely accepted and believed: Christ Jesus came into the world to save sinners. I am the worst of them, but it was for this very reason that God was merciful to me, in order that Christ Jesus might show His full patience in dealing with me, the worst of sinners, as an example for all those who would later believe in Him and receive eternal life. 1 Timothy 1:15-16 (From the Epistle for the Seventeenth Sunday After Pentecost)

The World

Two pair of scissors, one the kind used in kindergarten, the other a sharp pair; several pieces of paper of varying weights, including tissue paper and heavy cardboard that the good scissors will cut but the other pair will not.

Let's pretend I am doing a television commercial to show how good these scissors (expensive pair) are. Look, the scissors will cut paper (tissue paper). You know that's not so great. Even these scissors from the kindergarten class will cut that paper. But how about this (heavier) paper? (Continue to use both scissors to cut heavier paper until the inexpensive scissors will no longer cut.)

The real test was when I cut this heavy cardboard with the good scissors. The other scissors could not do it. Our Bible reading for today is like a TV commercial to tell us that Christ can save all sinners. And Paul says that he is like the heavy cardboard that only a good scissors can cut—he is such a bad sinner that only a great Savior could save him. Listen to the reading: "Christ Jesus came into the world to save sinners. I am the worst of them, but it was for this very reason that God was merciful to me, in order that Christ Jesus might show His full patience in dealing with me, the worst of sinners, as an example for all those who would later believe in Him and receive eternal life."

Paul had been an enemy of Christ. He had condemned all who followed Christ, and he had thrown Christians into jail. Yet this same Paul became a great missionary for Christ. To Paul, that showed how great Christ is. He is a Savior who can save anyone. Paul set himself as a good bad example.

And Paul says this example was given for us who later, that includes now, would believe in Christ as our Savior. He does not mean that we have to do some bad sin to show how great Christ is. In God's eyes we are all sinners who need a Savior. There is no difference in our guilt before God.

But in people's eyes there is a difference of guilt. We see some people as bad and some not so bad—like the difference in the thickness of these pieces of paper. But when we know that Christ can save the people who appear to be the worst, we also know He can save all the others. We don't have to pretend that we are better than others. We can admit we are sinners and yet know we have a Savior who can remove our sin.

Use the Right List

The Word

First of all, then, I urge that petitions, prayers, requests, and thanksgivings be offered to God for all men, for kings and all others who are in authority, that we may live a quiet and peaceful life, in entire godliness and proper conduct. This is good and it pleases God our Savior, who wants all men to be saved and to come to know the truth. 1 Timothy 2:1-4 (From the Epistle for the Eighteenth Sunday after Pentecost)

The World

Two grocery lists (on posters or show on an overhead projector). A: items for a child (candy, cokes, chips, etc.). B: items for a family (vegetables, meat, salt, etc.). Two prayer lists: C: "parents, friends, self, grandma." D: those on "C" plus: "enemies, hungry people in Africa, politicians, _____, _____, all people."

Have you ever used a prayer list? A prayer list is like a grocery list. It reminds you what to do. For example, this list (A) might remind you what you want to buy. But look at this list (B). The first list was for you. This one is for the family. Your mother would have made this list (B), but you might have made the other.

Now think about who you pray for. Your list might look like this (C). You may add names to this list but add only those for whom you have prayed in the last week.

Now look at this list (D). It includes all the names from your list, and also some more. This list could be very long—see the blank spaces? At the bottom, two words summarize the list: "all people." The first list was made by you. It includes the people you love and care about. The second list is God's list. It includes everyone He loves and cares about.

God tells us how He makes a prayer list for us to use. Our Bible reading says, "I urge that petitions, prayers, requests, and thanksgivings be offered to God for all men [that means all people], for kings and all others who are in authority, that we may live a quiet and peaceful life, in entire godliness and proper conduct. This is good and it pleases God our Savior, who wants all men [again, that's all people] to be saved and to come to know the truth."

The Bible reading gives you three reasons why you should pray for all people. First, and most important: God loves all people and wants all people to be saved. Christ gave Himself to be the Savior of all people. If we pray only for those whom we love, we might have a short list. If we pray for all whom God loves, we have a long list.

The second reason we pray for all people is that praying for some people helps other people. For example, if you pray for the president or others in authority, you are also praying for all the people that are under their authority. Also, if you pray for teachers, doctors, business people, police, parents, you are praying not only for those individuals but for all the people they work with.

Finally, we are to pray for all people because all people need our prayers. This list (D) shows us only a few. Notice that you don't have to know a person's name to pray. You can pray for many people because you know they are there. You know they need God's help, and you know God wants to help them. When you ask Him to help, He may ask you to help Him answer your prayer.

When you are praying, use a prayer list. But use the list that God made.

Can Others Tell Where You Are Going?

The Word

But you, man of God, avoid all these things. Strive for righteousness, godliness, faith, love, endurance, and gentleness. Run your best in the race of faith, and win eternal life for yourself; for it was to this life that God called you when you made your good profession of faith before many witnesses. 1 Timothy 6:11-12 (From the Epistle for the Nineteenth Sunday After Pentecost)

The World

A child and a pad of paper, pencil.

Robin is going to help me today; because we want to have a special kind of a race. In this race we want the rest of you to guess where Robin's finish line is. I'll write it on a piece of paper and give it to her (or whisper in the ear of a smaller child). (Give the child a goal, such as door, chair, etc., across the room.) Okay, Robin, on your mark, get set, go. (After she arrives at the goal) We all know what her goal is because she is there.

Paul tells Timothy about life and calls it a race. What he says also applies to us. Listen: "Run your best in the race of faith, and win eternal life for yourself; for it was to this life that God called you when you made your good profession of faith before many witnesses."

Notice that Paul tells Timothy to win eternal life. But remember, he also says that God called Timothy to that eternal life. Just as I gave Robin the goal so she knew where to go, God has given us a goal so we know how to live. Our life is like a race and the finish line is heaven.

But the race is not like the one that Robin ran before. It is more like this: Come back, Robin, and I will give you a different goal. (Give her another finish line in a different direction.) This time you can take only the steps that I tell you. First take one giant step. Now take three baby steps. (Continue to give limited steps until others will know where she is headed.)

In real life we have a difficult time getting to the finish line. We take only a few steps at a time. We take small steps. Our selfishness, our willingness to follow others instead of God, our lack of love for others, all these things, which can be called sin, keep us from being completely with God. But Paul says to keep trying. He knew about the things that try to make us quit the race. He said, "But avoid all those things. Strive for righteousness, godliness, faith, love, endurance, and gentleness."

Notice that in the second race Robin did not get to the goal yet. But all of you could tell where the goal was. She was headed toward it. If she would have gone over that way, or turned down there, we would not have known where she was going. Even though her limited, small steps kept her from getting to the goal right away, she was on her way.

And we are on the way in our race of faith. We need to stop to repent. We know that many temptations try to make us go other directions. But when we aim for the gifts that the Holy Spirit gives us through Christ, we are headed in the right direction. Strive for righteousness, godliness, faith, love, endurance, and gentleness—then you're on the right track.

God Was Ready for You

The Word

[God] saved us and called us to be His own people, not because of what we have done, but because of His own purpose and grace. He gave us this grace by means of Christ Jesus before the beginning of time, but now it has been revealed to us through the coming of our Savior, Christ Jesus. He has ended the power of death and through the Good News has revealed immortal life. 2 Timothy 1:9-10 (From the Epistle for the Twentieth Sunday After Pentecost)

The World

A plate of food (if possible use spaghetti, fried chicken, or french fries) and a napkin.

Jesus often said that He gave gifts to us in the same way that someone invites us to a fancy dinner. God is the host and we are the guests. He tells us to come to His house for a big meal. Our Bible reading includes an invitation from God. It says, "[God] saved us and called us to be His own people, not because of what we have done, but because of His own purpose and grace."

God invites us because He loves us. He is not paying us back for the time we invited Him to dinner. He is not having a dinner to sell something. He wants us to be with Him.

And here is the dinner. (Show plate.) You might be hungry now. Seeing this food will make you more hungry. But that's okay—just let your hunger help you remember how much you need the love and grace that God gives you in Christ.

However, if you were served this plate of food at God's place, you might be uncomfortable. If you were eating with God, you would want to use your best table manners. And even when you try hard, you might spill food. But look—God not only gave you the food. He also gave you a napkin. He knew you might spill something, or get some food on your hands or chin; so He gave

111

you a napkin to keep you from being embarrassed. In our spiritual life that napkin is the daily forgiveness of sin. When God calls us to His party, He forgives us. And He also continues to give us forgiveness in Christ.

It is important that the napkin was at our place when the dinner started. God did not wait until we made a mess and then look for a way to solve it. He loves us so much that He prepared the meal and the napkin for us. Notice what the rest of our Bible reading says, "He gave us this grace by means of Christ Jesus before the beginning of time, but now it has been revealed to us through the coming of our Savior, Christ Jesus. He has ended the power of death and through the Good News has revealed immortal life."

Before the beginning of time, even before we sinned, God prepared His grace for us in Christ Jesus. We did not see this grace clearly until Christ came to die for our sins and to give us eternal life. But when we received the gift of Christ, it was not a new gift. God had it for us from the beginning. He did not wait until we sinned to plan a way of salvation for us. As a host puts a napkin beside the plate in case it is needed, God, from the beginning, gave us grace in Christ Jesus. He was prepared for us.

When you sit down at a dinner and see a napkin, let it remind you of Christ. Even before you needed help, God gave it.

Christ Shares Your Life

The Word

This is a true saying: "If we have died with Him, we shall also live with Him. If we continue to endure, we shall also rule with Him. If we deny Him, He also will deny us. If we are not faithful, He remains faithful, because He cannot be false to Himself." 2 Timothy 2:11-13 (From the Epistle for the Twenty-first Sunday After Pentecost)

The World

Two large posters. On one draw a map with a major road called "Christ" and another called "You." Each road starts at the left. The two merge near the right and extend off the right side. The second map is the same except the roads meet near the left side and are together across the poster. On both maps have other, smaller roads intersecting the major highways.

From our Bible reading: "This is a true saying: 'If we have died with Him [that is Jesus], we shall also live with Him.'" The promise is that if we share Christ's death—which we have—He can share our death—which He will.

That promise can be seen on a map like this. See—one highway is called "Christ." The other is called "You"—that stands for each of us. These two highways meet at an intersection called "Death." When we meet at death, we continue, not as two separate highways, but as one and live forever together.

But our Bible reading gives us a promise even greater than the one you see on this map. It says, "If we continue to endure, we shall also rule with Him. If we deny Him, He also will deny us. If we are not afraid, He remains faithful, because He cannot be false to Himself."

This promise reminds us that we meet Christ before the time of our death. (Show second map.) See? The two highways merge when Christ becomes a part of your life on earth! Just as one

113

highway can have two route numbers, "Christ" and "You" merge to form one road. Your lives are together. You go past many intersections. This one is temptation—remember Christ shares your temptations, but He does it without sin. You cross the intersection of sorrow—but you are not alone. There are many other intersections that cause joy, pain, disappointment. But Christ is with you at each one. And when you come to death, you are not separated from Christ. The two highways continue together.

The text has a warning for us. It says if we deny Christ, He will deny us. To deny Him is to take our life off His road. He will not go astray with us. Instead He will call us back to Him. Even in the warning there is a promise. It says even though we are unfaithful He will be faithful. He will always stay on the highway leading to eternal life. He will always call us to come back to Him.

By your baptism your life and Christ's life have been brought together like two highways. When you see two route numbers on the same signpost, think of one of them as saying "Christ" and the other one as having your name. You travel through life with Him.

A Gift with a Purpose

The Word

All Scripture is inspired by God and is useful for teaching the truth, rebuking error, correcting faults, and giving instruction for right living, so that the man who serves God may be fully qualified and equipped to do every kind of good work. 2 Timothy 3:16-17 (From the Epistle for the Twenty-second Sunday After Pentecost)

The World

A pocket calculator and a Bible.

Have you ever used one of these? (Show the calculator.) It is fun to play with, but it is not a toy. It is an adding machine—see? (Do an addition problem.) It also subtracts, multiplies, and divides (show other functions). If you know how to use a machine like this, you can do all kinds of math problems without difficulty.

What if someone gave you a calculator like this and you played with it for a while, then put it in a drawer and didn't use it? That would be a waste. If you only used the calculator as a toy and never used it in any of the ways that it could help, you have wasted a valuable gift.

Maybe you don't have a calculator, but you do have one of these (the Bible). The Bible can also do many things for you. It includes an instruction manual that tells you how to use it. The Bible reading for today says, "All Scripture is inspired by God and is useful for teaching the truth, rebuking error, correcting faults, and giving instruction for right living." Just like the calculator, the Bible can do many things. First and most important, the Bible tells you the truth of Jesus Christ. It shows you that you have a Savior who loves you and keeps you with Him.

115

The Bible also rebukes errors and corrects faults. I'm afraid that often we use the Bible to rebuke other people for their errors and to correct their faults. But the Bible is intended for us—to correct our faults and to rebuke our errors. It also shows us how we can live as Christian people. The Scripture tells us how to live with others who also believe in Christ and with those who do not.

But if the Bible is to help us do these things, we must use it. We can't just say, "That's a great book. It is God's Holy Word," then put it on the shelf. The Bible is not a magic book that helps us because we have it in our homes. The book is to be read, shared, and followed. The Bible reading assures us that the Scripture equips us to do the work that God has planned for us.

We admit that we often fail to do the things that we should. We don't serve God as He told us to. We don't help other people as we would like to be helped. When we need help, let's reach for the Book that tells us about Christ. Read again of His love for us. Hear Him correct us and forgive us. See how He loves others and gives us a way to love them too. Then we are using the power the Holy Spirit gives us through the Gospel.

An Everyday Faith for a Special Day

The Word

As for me, the hour has come for me to be sacrificed; the time is here for me to leave this life. I have done my best in the race, I have run the full distance, I have kept the faith. And now the prize of victory is waiting for me, the crown of righteousness which the Lord, the righteous Judge, will give me on that Day. 2 Timothy 4:6-8a (From the Epistle for the Twenty-third Sunday after Pentecost)

The World

A newspaper and a volume from an encyclopedia set.

In the Bible reading you just heard, St. Paul told you he was ready to die. He wrote this message near the end of his life while he was in prison. When he looked back over his life, he was happy. He said he had done his best in the race. He made it the full distance. And when he looked to the future, he was also happy, because he knew he would go to heaven to be with Christ, his righteous Judge.

St. Paul is a good example for us when we think about our own death. A person who can be happy when he thinks about both the past and future can die happy. And Paul tells us his secret—he has kept the faith. His faith that Christ was his Savior was a part of his past. Because Christ died for him Paul knew his sins were forgiven. Because Christ rose again Paul knew he also would live after death. Paul could be happy as he neared death not just because he had faith when he died. But also because he had faith when he lived.

Look at this comparison. This book (the encyclopedia) is like some many of you have in your homes. All of you have them in your classrooms. This is an important book when you need the information in it. This is volume K. If you need to know

117

anything about a subject that starts with K, you would need this book. Of course, a book like this may be in your house for weeks or even months without anyone using it. But when you need special information, you need an encyclopedia.

Some people think of faith like an encyclopedia. They keep it on hand, on the shelf in their minds, for the special times when they think about death. Then faith tells them that Christ had died for them and they do not need to be afraid to die.

But faith in Christ offers us more than a way to die. It also gives us a way to live. Faith is more like this newspaper. The paper has many messages in it. Here is the latest news, editorials, sports, stockmarket reports, comics, want ads, advertisements for movies and groceries. And much more. The paper has so much news we need a new one every day.

Our faith in Christ also applies to all parts of our lives. Not only does it help us prepare to die, but our faith also helps us live with ourselves and with other people. Our faith tells us Christ is with us when we are lonely or afraid. It strengthens us when we are weak or tempted. It humbles us when we are proud. It comforts us when we are scared. It fills us with joy and happiness.

Because Paul kept the faith, not just for the day he died, but in all parts of his life, he could die happy. We can too. Don't keep some special faith reserved like an encyclopedia on a shelf. Have a faith like a newspaper that is new every day and applies to everything you do.

Being Thankful for People

The Word

We must thank God at all times for you, brothers. It is right for us to do so, because your faith is growing so much and the love each of you has for the others is becoming greater. 2 Thessalonians 1:3 (From the Epistle for the Twenty-fourth Sunday After Pentecost)

The World

An apple and something to represent an apple tree (a twig from a tree, a picture, or a sketch made on a large sheet of poster paper).

Please think of people for whom you are thankful. Look at your thankfulness this way: I am glad that I know _____. Then fill in the blank with as many names as you want. You may list friends first—the people you have fun with. When you think about the list, you may add parents and even brothers and sisters. Parents will probably start their lists by naming their children. You may even add teachers, neighbors, other relatives.

Making such a list is a way to say thanks for having friends and family. You could add other things to a thanksgiving list. For example, you could say you are thankful to have this (the apple); if you like apples, that is. And you may be thankful for money, a home, clothes, and many other things. But there is a difference between thanking God for what you have and for your friends and family. Listen to what St. Paul says in our Bible reading: "We must thank God at all times for you, brothers. It is right for us to do so, because your faith is growing so much and the love each of you has for the others is becoming greater."

Notice the reason Paul is thankful for his friends—because their faith in Christ is growing and because the love they have for each other is becoming greater. In other words, he is thankful not just for the people but also for what is happening to them. He is

119

thankful not only that they know Christ as their Savior but that they are learning to trust Him even more. He is thankful that his friends love him and each other but also that their love is growing stronger. Instead of being thankful just for the apple (show it), he is thankful for the tree (show twig or picture) that produces more apples.

We can learn two important lessons from this Bible reading. First, being thankful for your friends and family is more important than being thankful for the things such as food, clothing, and the like, you have. Sure, thank God for those things. But be even more thankful for those you love and those who love you, because their friendship is not something like an apple that you can use once but like a tree that produces more apples.

Secondly, remember you can grow in love to be an even greater blessing in the lives of other people. Christ has given you His love so you can love others. The Holy Spirit helps your faith grow so that through you others can learn about Jesus as the Savior. You can love your family and friends even more, and you can expand your love to include more people.

Pack a Heartful of Courage

The Word

May our Lord Jesus Christ Himself, and God our Father, who loved us and in His grace gave us eternal courage and a good hope, fill your hearts with courage and make you strong to do and say all that is good. 2 Thessalonians 2:16-17 (From the Epistle for the Twenty-fifth Sunday After Pentecost)

The World

A small shaving or cosmetic kit, an overnight bag, and a large suitcase.

In our Bible reading for today St. Paul and some of his friends say good-by to the people at a church. They loved the people of this church very much, but Paul knows he will not see them again. So he tells the people to fill their hearts with courage. He also tells them that he has a special kind of courage in mind— the courage that comes from Christ, who loves all people.

Can you imagine yourself filling your heart with the courage Christ gives you? Remember the courage comes from Christ, who loved you so much He died for you and took away all your sin. Your courage is based on His resurrection from the dead, that assures you you will live with Him forever.

After you've filled your heart with that courage, does it look like this (the small kit)? If I packed this kit for a trip, you would know that I didn't plan to go very far or stay very long. The kit has room only for a tooth brush and razor. But if I packed for a trip with this (the overnight bag), you would know that I planned a longer trip. This bag would carry extra socks and shirts. But if you saw me pack this (the suitcase), you would know that I planned a long trip. This suitcase has room for several changes of clothes, shoes, and anything I'd need for a long trip.

Now, which of these three cases represents your heart? Do you have enough courage to last just a little while—so you could pack it in this kit? Or would you need this overnight bag?

Jesus would say, "Hey, I offered you more courage than that. Remember I died for you and I'm alive again. That's enough for a long trip—one that will never end. Use the big suitcase and I'll fill it with courage."

If you know that Christ has eternal life waiting for you; then it is worthwhile to pack the big suitcase full of courage. You don't need just enough to get through school, or through a job, or even just through death. You need enough to last not just 50 or 60 or 100 years, but you need enough of God's love in Christ to last you forever. And the Holy Spirit gives it to you.

The courage that Christ packs in your heart helps you live on earth as well as know you will go to heaven. God's courage helps you say and do the right things. Remember how often you'd like to be brave enough not to hit back with your fists, but you are afraid people will think you are a sissy if you don't. Remember the times you needed courage not to say nasty things to someone who did something to hurt you. Or remember the time you could have told someone that Jesus' love was for everyone, but you weren't sure you could do it. When those things happen again, remember the big suitcase. Your heart is like this suitcase. God has filled it with enough courage to help you say and do the right things now and to know you will live with Him forever.

Are You Waiting or Working?

The Word

While we were with you we told you, "Whoever does not want to work is not allowed to eat." We say this because we hear that there are some people among you who live lazy lives, who do nothing except meddle in other people's business. In the name of the Lord Jesus Christ we command these people and warn them: they must lead orderly lives and work to earn their own living, But you, brothers, must not get tired of doing good. 2 Thessalonians 3:10-13 (From the Epistle for the Twenty-sixth Sunday After Pentecost)

The World

Eleven sheets of 8½ x 11 paper, each with one of the following on it: "6," "+," " -," "6," "=," "12," "0," "Grace," "Christ's return," "Work for Christ," "Wait for Christ." Roll of tape.

An arithmetic lesson will help us understand today's Bible reading. Let me put this math problem up and see if you can solve it. (Tape the following on a wall or have five children hold them: "6," leave a space, "6," "=," leave a space.) The answer? You don't know because you haven't see all of the problem. You can't know what goes here (last space), until you know what goes here (second space). If I put this ("-") here (second space), the answer is "0." But if I put this ("+") here the answer is "12."

Now listen to another kind of problem in the Bible reading. It says: "While we were with you we told you: 'Whoever does not want to work is not allowed to eat.' We say this because we hear that there are some people among you who live lazy lives, who do nothing except meddle in other people's business. In the name of the Lord Jesus Christ we command these people and warn them: they must lead orderly lives and work to earn their own living. But you, brothers, must not get tired of doing good."

The problem is not just with lazy people. It is with lazy Christians—people who use their faith in Christ as an excuse for doing nothing. We can see it as a math problem. Christians know Christ has saved them by grace. (Put "Grace" in place of the first "6" and remove "+.") We also know that Christ is coming to take us to live with Him. (Put "Christ's Return" in place of second "6.") Now what's the answer.

Of course, the answer depends on what you put here (second space). If I put in the minus (do it), we say that we are saved and Christ is coming to get us soon, so the answer is "Wait for Christ." The people to whom Paul wrote were waiting. They didn't want to work. They depended on Jesus; so they'd sit around and wait for Him to show up.

But Paul says they were wrong. We should see God's grace in Christ and His promise to return with a plus sign between them (do it). God has given us both His grace and His promise to return. If we add them together, rather than subtract one from the other, we get a different answer. It is: "Work for Jesus."

Because God has saved us—because He is coming to take us to be with Him; we can work for Him. We can work to provide for ourselves and others. Notice the Bible does not say, "Whoever cannot work is not allowed to eat." It is, "Whoever does not want to work is not allowed to eat." Some cannot work. But we can work for them so when we eat they can also eat. When we know that God's grace in Christ is a part of us and that He adds His promise to come back for us, we will not get tired of doing good for others.

Get the Protection That Works

The Word

So when what is mortal has been clothed with what is immortal, and when what will die has been clothed with what cannot die, then the Scripture will come true: "Death is destroyed; victory is complete!" 1 Corinthians 15:54 (From the Epistle for the Twenty-seventh Sunday After Pentecost)

The World

A plastic sack of cookies and a metal container large enough to hold the cookies.

Do you know it is time to mail Christmas gifts? If you want to send a gift to a missionary, someone in the military, or anyone else who lives overseas, you have to mail the gift now.

Suppose you wanted to send this sack of cookies to someone who lived in Africa or Europe. That should be simple. Put a name tag on it and mail it. But you know that wouldn't work. The cookies would be crushed and the bag would break. If you want to send the cookies, you first have to put them in a container like this. Then the container could be wrapped and mailed.

I'm going to read today's Bible reading as though it were written about cookies. Remember this isn't what the Bible says, but by hearing it speak about the cookies, you'll understand what is says about you. "So when the breakable has been put in what is unbreakable, and when what will be crushed is stored in a crushproof container, then the promise is true: 'You can mail the cookies overseas!' "

But that part of the Bible is actually talking about us. It says we are mortals—that means we will die. Just as the cookies would be crushed if mailed, we will die sometime. All of our lives we have to think about death. We have to wonder if death will destroy us. We wonder if we will be punished after we die. Or we wonder if death will be the end of us.

Just as the breakable cookies needed an unbreakable box, we who are capable of death need a container that cannot be killed. So that we do not have to live with the fear of death, we need something to protect us from death. We need something to take away the threat of punishment.

And we have it. Listen to what the Bible reading really says: "So when what is mortal (that is, going to die) has been clothed with what is immortal (that is, not going to die), and when what will die has been clothed with what cannot die, then the Scripture will come true: 'death is destroyed; victory is complete!' "

Christ is the container that protects us from death. Because He faced death on the cross and destroyed death 3 days later by rising from His grave, Christ is immortal. He will not die again. He has a new life.

And Christ invites us to come to Him. He tells us to be in Him when we face the time of our death. Then our death can be like His death—temporary. Death will not be punishment for us. Death will not be the end of our lives. Like Jesus, we will be raised to a new life.

See What Can't Be Seen

Christ is the visible likeness of the invisible God. Colossians 1:15a (From the Epistle for the Last Sunday After Pentecost)

The World

A flashlight and a picture of Jesus.

The Bible reading for today says something that seems impossible. It says we can see something that can't be seen. Listen: "Christ is the visible likeness of the invisible God." We can see Christ. So in Him we can see God, who is invisible.

Of course we can see Christ. This is a picture of Him. All of you would recognize the picture. But the picture isn't Christ. No one took a picture of the Savior with a camera, and no one who saw Him painted a picture of Him or told us what He looks like. Besides, any picture of Christ shows Him in the likeness of people. Pictures show that He became like us. The Bible reading tells us that in Christ we see the likeness of God.

Let's look for another way to see Christ. This illustration will help. See this flashlight? It has batteries in it and the batteries contain power. We can't see the power but we can know it is there. The power is invisible, like God, but when I turn the flashlight on, the power becomes visible. Christ is like this light. He makes the power of God visible for us. See it in the light.

You can see this light when you look at it. But there is another way you can see the light. See, when I shine the light away from you on the wall, you can see the light there. What you see is the wall, but the light on the wall makes a difference. The power from those batteries makes the light that changes the way we see the wall.

We also see Christ in our lives today when the power of God

shines in our lives. First, look at yourself in the light of Christ. Christ is your Savior. He has given you the power of God's love and forgiveness. He has given you eternal life. Christ's light shining on you makes you different. His light shows you are forgiven. It shows you live in hope. Though you have never seen God, in the same way you see me, you can see God in your life. Just as you see the power of these batteries on my face when I shine the flashlight on myself, the light of Christ shining on you shows how God changes your life.

The light of Christ also shines on other people around you. You can see the power of God in people who also receive Christ's light in their life. You can see God made visible in people who help others, in those who tell others the good news of Christ as Savior of the world, in those who feed hungry people and take care of sick people.

Think how Christ has changed the world by changing the people who live in the world. Let His power be seen in you so others may see Christ, the visible likeness of the invisible God, in you. Also look for Christ in others. See God made visible in the lives of others who also receive and reflect the light of Christ.